MW00437946

TRADE
SECRETS

TRADE SECRETS

MONEYMAKING AND TIMESAVING TIPS AND ADVICE FOR WRITERS

Eva Shaw

PARAGON HOUSE
New York

First edition, 1993

Published in the United States by

Paragon House
90 Fifth Avenue
New York, New York 10011

Copyright © 1993 by Eva Shaw

All rights reserved. No part of this book may be
reproduced, in any form, without written permission
from the publishers, unless by a reviewer who wishes
to quote brief passages.

Manufactured in the United States of America

Library of Congress Cataloging-in-Publication Data

Shaw, Eva
    Trade secrets : moneymaking and timesaving tips and advice for
writers / Eva Shaw.
      p.   cm.
   ISBN 1-55778-584-8
   1. Authorship. I. Title.
PN151.S55   1993
808'.02—dc20   92-39003
                                  CIP

Dedication

To my biggest fan.

Contents

SECTION 2: THE BUCK STOPS HERE

CONTENTS

SECTION 3: HOUR POWER—SAVE TIME, INCREASE
YOUR PRODUCTIVITY

SECTION 4: THE POWER OF THE PRINTED WORD—
READING, WRITING, AND REJECTION

SECTION 5: MAKING YOUR NAME KNOWN IN ALL THE
RIGHT PLACES

Acknowledgments

Through my writing life, I have had the profound opportunity to swap trade secrets with smart, funny, sharp, outrageous, articulate, intelligent, and/or loony writers, novelists, agents, editors, and publishers. Our fun, fascinating, totally unpredictable careers have never been monotonous, never the same two days in a row. That's why we all love it, right?

Many graciously gave me their tips, suggestions, opinions, and sometimes the time of day. Special thanks for their comments, advice, ideas, and use of material to Linda Abel, Cathy Colman, Patricia C. Gallagher, Nancy C. Grant, Wendy Haskett, Bert Holtje, M. Sue Lasbury, Ali Lassen, John Lee, Cory J Meachem, Liz Palika, Milt Pierce, Pam Posey, Harriet Schechter, Ted Schwarz, and George Sheldon.

Thank you, also, to all those writers I've met and spoken with at writers' conferences—from San Diego to New York City and plenty of places between. You were the reason and the stimulus for *Trade Secrets* because you asked questions. From these questions has come the advice available herein, ready and waiting.

My literary agent, Bert Holtje, once more has proven that he's the best agent in the world, and with this like other projects he encouraged me to submit the proposal for a book on advice to writers and added his pithy wisdom. PJ Dempsey and Chris O'Connell, my editors at Paragon House, and their staff again checked all the i's and t's. They deftly shook the chaff from the literary wheat and helped me to produce a polished book filled to the brim with trade secrets.

Thank you to all.

Introduction

Stockbrokers, seamstresses, bricklayers, and bakers all have one thing in common: To make more money and stretch what they have, they use trade secrets, handed down from broker to broker, baker to baker.

As writers of fiction and nonfiction, we often work alone with little opportunity to swap tricks and tactics, secrets and suggestions about writing. Yet we spend hours trying to decipher what the public, agents, editors, and publishers want to buy and read now and in the future. We spend even more time producing glorious golden prose and then knock ourselves silly with self-promotion—*all without knowing exactly how to do it*. And it's often done while being isolated from the rest of the writing world.

That's where *Trade Secrets* comes in. Imagine this book as a group of ultrasuccessful writers sitting in your office telling you everything you really need to know to make it. We're not talking about the things Mrs. Bubble told you in Creative Writing 101 or rigid rhetoric of freshman

English. This is the nuts and bolts stuff all those Mrs. Bubbles didn't know like:

- How to get at least 15 percent off everything you buy at the stationery store
- How writing for the confession markets could be a gold mine
- How you can have all the advantages of a FAX machine without buying one
- How "Literary Darwinism" can work for you
- How to unstick the "Catch-22" of getting an agent

If you're looking for help to write a sentence, punctuate a paragraph, or use the right syntax, this isn't the book for you. But if you want to make more money, you're in the right place at the right time.

Trade Secrets is a practical course in success, savvy, and strategies so you can be a more effective and efficient writer. Without sounding like a hyped-up TV ad, this book comes with a guarantee: If you utilize the tips and advice in this book along with plenty of all-American roll-up-your-sleeves energy, you will make more money and have more at the end of the year. The suggestions tell you how to do it, but the elbow work is up to you. Apply and recycle the tips and suggestions, modify them, make them your own, and use them to build the career of your dreams.

I've been a working, money-making writer for over fourteen years with more than one thousand credits. All the trade secrets here are real ones I have used, seen in action, and/or adopted. They have been refined and tested; every single one works. You have my word as a comrade in print.

Whether you're a seasoned pro or a newcomer, you'll quickly see that some of the items are inserted because, as working writers, we need to have our memories jogged. We need to know how to accomplish more in less time and how to make more money doing the same amount of work. Some of the advice is included because I have been asked about the topics while giving lectures and seminars on writing at conferences and colleges. Topics that I think are fundamental to any good writing business are presented here from my years of attending the College of Trial and Blunder—"courses" you won't have to take if you digest this information.

Even those who have been in the business for some time, as well as beginning writers, get hungry for practical information that's not being presented in the current cluster of writers' books. That's what you'll find within these pages: realistic how-to, do-it-better, do-it-now material and ways you can take it to the bank.

Was it Benjamin Franklin who said, "A penny saved is a penny earned"? The truth be known, pennies don't count much anymore (I'm sorry, too, Ben), but dollars still do. Therefore, my main thrust is on saving bucks, *your* bucks. When it all comes down to the bottom line, we are in business. Don't let anyone's preconceived opinion of literary integrity and the artistry of writing keep you from making a living. You can make money writing—you can make *lots* of money writing. And money is good; it provides choices, from which book to buy to which political party (or cause) to support.

I work for money (healthy doses of ego gratification are an excellent by-product) and my work is "commercial" as opposed to "cerebral" or literary. I've designed my writing business in that way because, while penning *The Great American Novel* has an elusive, mouth-watering appeal, I can't pay the power company or support my local supermarket without selling my work. To some that might sound materialistic, yet the reason I've revealed this fact is that if you are writing for strictly the joy of it, this book may not be right for you. However, don't discount the information until you've flipped through some of the pages and learned a thing or three. Even literary types want to pay bills, invest in mutual funds, and take vacations.

The concepts you'll find within these pages work. They're written short, sweet, and snappy because who among us has time for a lengthy volume of literary wisdom? Really. If you have enough time to pour over a verbose dissertation on writing, there are plenty of long-winded books at the library. And if you don't want better ways to work, you're probably independently wealthy and writing is a hobby. That's okay. Gently pass this book on to a writer who needs it and wants to make a living.

Using these trade secrets will boost your achievement rate in sales, improve time management, and ensure that your psyche is satisfied. Not all the recommendations tell you how to make more money. You'll find some that disclose how to stretch your well-earned dollars. Some give ideas that will help you put a twist on your current methods, fine-tune your PR, set up a networking system, and do it better.

The Athenian orator Demosthenes said, "Small opportunities are often the beginning of great enterprises." This book may feel little, but inside are trade secrets that could triple the money you make (and keep) each year. It all depends on you.

Trade Secrets shares years of experience and provides answers to the most knotty problems. To sprinkle a little spice, I've added favorite tips from other writers in associated fields, with a few from agents and publishers thrown in for good measure.

Trade Secrets is not a how-to-format-a-more-absorbing-sentence book, but rather one filled with intelligent methods and concrete tactics to put to use immediately with ways to make a writer's career thrive in a recession and out. *Trade Secrets* also has a few warnings on how to avoid snags and pitfalls of the profession.

Read the book as you see fit. A little here, a little there, or everything in one sitting. And when you're finished and want to share your best bit of advice, write me in care of Paragon House.

SECTION
1

Getting Ready, Staying Motivated, and Making It as a Writer

Among people who do not make their living writing there's a misconception that all it takes to be a writer is a pencil (or computer) and paper. No unusual talent. No real knowledge of grammar, organization, or composition. No previous experience. No burning desire. No business sense. No nothing.

The truth, as we writers know, is that more than a wish to write is required to write magazine articles and books. Along with creativity, it takes a heap of perseverance, an overabundance of patience, and a whole lot of practice arranging those words to make a marketable manuscript. The writing life is so downright habit forming some of us think it should come with a warning label: YOU MAY BECOME ADDICTED. Once you are, there's no rest until you see your byline on that first published article, column, or book.

Sure there's frustration; it's part of the game. And as the cliche goes, if you can't take the heat, get away from the computer . . . or something like that. Even though the threat of disappointment constantly lurks at the mailbox, there are ways to sidestep the obstacles, jump start your career, stay motivated, and make it as a writer. *And* do it in a faster and more pleasurable way.

That's where the trade secrets in this section come in handy. Those not in the know ignore the fact that, whether you specialize in fiction or nonfiction, there are better ways to write, get published, and continue to build a career. Let's look at what you need to know to get started.

1.1 What You Need to Know to Get Started in Writing

Don't be intimidated by the supercreative people who create three-dimensional images with phrases that make you seesaw between a guffaw and the urge to rip your heart to shreds, or those who can whip out a nail-biting plot line in the time it takes you to jot down a grocery list.

In the writing classes I've attended and in some at which I've spoken, I've met them, too: the truly creative writers who can't seem to finish a piece of writing, let alone market their work. I envy their ability to capture golden words that go from mind to paper; but in the big picture of life, the writers who make it are disciplined, meet deadlines, sell their work, and continue to write, often in the face of rejection. The ultraartistic types often never make it past the fifty-yard line while we're standing next to the goal post.

Talent is great, but stick-to-ed-ness brings home the bucks. That trait and desire are all you need for a career as a writer.

1.2 Literary Darwinism

In this time of economic crunch, only the strongest writers are left. That's great news for the savviest, swiftest, and most serious because when the economy officially turns around (not just the corners we're enjoying now), those of us who have stuck it out will be well entrenched in our field. Survivors? Perhaps, and considerably smarter about marketing our writing.

1.3 Writing as a Second Career

Are you a retired person, a computer whiz, a disabled teenager, a parent or a therapist? If you're any of these things, to name a few, you are an expert. Use your expertise to write as a second career.

A writer who spent twenty years as a bookkeeper is writing a book on bookkeeping methods for the small business owner. A fire marshal is also the publisher of a fire protection trade journal (a magazine published specifically for people in one profession). A school teacher writes and sells oodles of fillers and short humor to magazines like *Reader's Digest*.

1.4   Are You an Expert?

Writing instructors often tell us to write what we know from our experience. Although that may not qualify you as an expert, your expertise can be the starting point for your article or book. From my experience in gourmet cooking classes, I wrote a number of articles and interviews about food and chefs. As a voracious reader of health material, I compiled information on health newsletters. Start with the education or background you have, add a new twist, interview *real* experts, compile information from numerous (accredited) sources, and then write a book or article.

1.5   So You Want to Join a Writers' Group?

Three Dog Night sang that one is the loneliest number. That's the feeling of some writers and why they reach out to critique and writers' groups.

The most important questions regarding critique groups are: Why do you want to join? Are you searching for a second opinion? Are you lonely? Do you want to network? Are you looking for a writing soul mate? These are all bona fide purposes; just make sure your needs are met.

And consider these guidelines:

- Can you take advice on your work? Can you disagree with a critique of your work without becoming hostile?
- Have you read the work of some of the writers in the group you plan to join? Is it the same or slightly above the caliber of your own work?
- Do you respect the people you'll be meeting with?
- Are you comfortable in their presence?
- Are their meetings convenient? Are they organized?
- Are they professional in their discussions of other writers' work?
- Would joining a large, national organization with monthly meetings and specific workshops be better than an intimate group?

1.6   Start a Writing Group of Your Own

Is it possible to start and continue a writing group on your own? Yes. But it takes work and enthusiasm from the members, and initially someone must be in charge of the organizational requirements. It works best to have a group writing in one specialty: mysteries, romances, nonfiction, humor, etc.

As you begin, invite people who are willing to make a commitment to an on-going group. Make the first meeting informal. Meet at a coffee house or restaurant, exchange a certain number of pages of whatever you're working on, then meet again in two weeks to hear the critique. Most groups meet once a month at someone's house and for a specific length of time.

The up side is that you'll instantly receive relevant appraisal. The down side is that each member must continually strive to keep the discussion germane to writing, and not let it degenerate into a bitch session that wastes time and energy.

1.7   Make the Most of Writers' Conferences

If you've never attended a writers' conference, treat yourself as soon as possible. For those who go to conferences, there are some considerations that will allow you to get the most from those hours. Here are tips to get the maximum amount of information in a limited amount of time:

• Find a conference in a location that's convenient and affordable. The conference's cost should be deductible (but you need income to deduct it from).

• Check for "hidden" costs (e.g. Will you have a long distance to travel? Will you have to stay in a hotel? Are meals included? Who will care for the kids or the cats when you're gone?).

• Read the brochure carefully. Are the speakers and seminars right for your writing specialty? I'd feel like a fish out of water at a science fiction writing conference.

• What are the credentials of the speakers? Are they people you know and admire, writers you've read?

• Why are you going to the conference? To meet fellow

writers, to learn about specific techniques (like dialogue, writing a book proposal), or to network with literary agents and publishers?

• If there is an agent or editor or noted writer you specifically would like to meet, write to the individual well before the conference. Let him or her know that you're looking forward to meeting. A creative writing teacher took this trade secret and ran with it. Planning to attend a conference in the Lake Tahoe area of California, she wrote three editors and an agent from one of the big literary agencies. "They loved the idea that I had written to introduce myself. It worked extremely well." So well, in fact, she had two editors and an agent clamoring for the rest of her manuscript.

The brochure should provide all this information, and if you still have questions—and you probably will—call for more facts. You might also try to locate a writer who has attended the same conference for a personal view.

1.8 Plan Your Strategy When You Attend a Writers' Conference

If you hope to pique the interest of an agent or editor with your manuscript, make sure it's polished and you include an SASE when handing over the material.

If you have the opportunity to sign up for a personal conference, write down your questions or have a list of potential topics of your work. Be sure to bring a tape recorder or make notes of the conference.

Have your business cards ready and get a card from each and every person you meet—especially those agents and editors—so you can follow-up with a note or your manuscript.

Plan your schedule carefully and jot down or highlight the workshops you plan to attend. If two of the most desirable workshops are happening at the same time, you may be able to get a tape of one and sit in the other. Be sure to ask for handouts at both workshops.

Network with other writers and ask about the workshops they've attended that day. If one or two sound extremely interesting, buy the tapes.

Writers' conferences are excellent places to network with other writers, but remember, you are there to learn. Spend time listening to the experts; chat with others after the conference is over.

1.9   Should You Take a Creative Writing Class at a College?

Most community colleges and universities have creative writing classes. Some, such as for senior citizens, are free. Most are extremely valuable to build confidence and provide a writer with a safe environment to write, read, and develop talent.

However, if you choose to attend creative writing classes, know when you've had enough, whether that's one semester or six. Don't allow the course to become an excuse for never progressing or selling your work. As an adult learner, you'll advance quicker than the "regular" college students because you have an immediate need for the information. Use it and write. Writing is the best teacher.

1.10 Writing as a Team Occupation

In the "two-heads-are-better-than-one" category, working with a writing partner can double your income. How so? If your partner is strong on grammar and composition and your strengths lay in interviewing and dialogue, you may have a match made in best-seller heaven. Select a partner with care; you should both have the similar dedication, work habits, time for the projects and goals.

Writing with a partner also works well if one of you is the writer and the other a legitimate expert. For example, you might write with a doctor who researches cures for cancer or with the president of an investment firm. While these individuals write well enough, a writer of your calibre will be able to get their messages out, make some money for both of you, and boost your writing career. Formalize your relationship with a good contract.

1.11 Talking Terms

Every trade, including writing, has its own jargon. Strange terms and terminologies are used in *Writer's Digest* or in a magazine's writers guidelines. Here's what some of them mean.

SASE: Self-addressed, stamped envelope. Whether you see this in guidelines or not, it behooves you to include an SASE with your query or proposal. An SASE doesn't guarantee that should your material be refused you'll get it back, but if you don't include one, you won't. If you work on a computer, format and save your name and address in envelope style on your hard disk and print out a number of pre-addressed envelopes when you have a few spare minutes.

SASP: Self-addressed, stamped postcard. Since most writers now work on computers, many are sending SASP instead of SASE. Sure this saves a little postage, but if an editor wants to send you something (such as a contract), a post card isn't going to do the trick and could slow the process.

IRC: International Reply Coupon. Like a uniglobal postage stamp, this is available at the post office. Your good old American stamps aren't going to work outside the States and IRCs are the answer. If you are contacting a foreign publisher or magazine and they ask that you include IRCs, do so. But I've found that most foreign publishers and magazine editors very kindly send guidelines and return unwanted articles without cost to you.

Query: A query, in writer's dialect, is a letter to inquire if a topic is of interest to a magazine or book publisher. Writers query before sending everything *except* fillers, humor, poetry, and opinion pieces.

Spec: This means an article is written on speculation,

with no promises, but with an opportunity, nonetheless. Magazine writers sometimes shy away from writing on spec because there are no guarantees that the material will be purchased. My thought is the opposite: I know that my work is good and my writing is marketable, and that I've written on my topic with a new twist. I know before I submit the article on spec that it will be right for the magazine because I've done the necessary "homework" (researching and reviewing the topic as well as the magazine). Therefore, in the beginning of a relationship with a magazine's editor, I'll write on spec. Spec is a good investment.

On assignment: When an article topic has been assigned, you've agreed to the terms of the assignment and signed a contract to produce the manuscript.

Electronic submission: Using a modem to submit your manuscript or submitting it on disk. Ten years ago, it was prophesied that by now we'd all be working on computers, and that the printed word would be dead. It didn't happen. A number of magazines and wire services say they'll take electronic submissions, but caution here: ask first. Publishing is still working with paper; submitting work this way is slowly being accepted but not as fast as was thought.

Mss and Ms: Manuscripts.

Tear sheet: A copy of the article as it appeared in a magazine. You may be asked to send clips or tear sheets of your work to show your writing style.

Word length: Most manuscripts have the estimated word length on the first page. Let the word counter on your computer do it for you. If you use a typewriter and have a lengthy manuscript, count the words on three pages, divide by three, and find the average. Multiply it by the number of pages in the manuscript and deduct for half pages (such as at the end of the article/book). Generally, publishers want the closest round number, and remember, they can count too. If you're asked for a 2,000-word article, don't fudge and submit 1,700. That 2,000-word piece is needed to fill a specific section and 1,700 is going to look too short. Same goes if you run over the specified amount.

Kill fee: The money you will receive if an assigned article is not used. Normally a kill fee is one half of the contracted amount.

1.12   What Genre Are You Writing In?

A genre is a class or category of writing. For example, romance writing, cookbooks, thrillers, and business books are each in their own genre. Some genres have "nicknames." Romances are called "bodice rippers," shoot 'em up action books are often called "boy books," and Agatha Christie–style mysteries where there are plenty of plot twists but little gushing blood are referred to as "cozies."

Ethnic might mean writing for the black reader, the Jewish reader, or the reader who has roots in Transylvania. The slice-of-life genre is home-spun common sense. Tom

Bodett, Erma Bombeck, and Andy Rooney combine slice-of-life with humor and do so with style.

Looking at *Writer's Market,* here are the definitions of typical magazine entries:

Arts and entertainment: The newest, the trendiest, the most intriguing news in the full spectrum that we call culture, from Blue Grass Music to banned books.

Consumer: Exposé, investigative, and how-to also fall into this genre.

Fashion and trends: What's hot and what's not. If you're psychic or have your finger on world trends, these timely pieces are incredibly popular.

General interest: Just about anything that doesn't fit into one of the other categories.

Interview/profile: An interview or personality sketch of someone whom readers of that specific publication would like to know more about.

Health, diet, and fitness: Often written by the lay writer, these articles are more easily sold when coauthored by a medical doctor or other specialist. *However,* you can focus on a topic and interview a number of professionals to prove your thesis.

Historic/nostalgic: Depending on the scope of the magazine (which you should investigate first before submitting a query), this may mean Americana or the early days of flight, growing up in Brooklyn or the impact of *Leave It to Beaver* on our adolescence.

Humor: Funny stuff. Again, how funny and in which amusing direction depends on the magazine. Writing humor for *Bridal Guide* will be different from writing humor for *Bird Watcher's Digest*. Sometimes humor stretches into other genres. I wrote an article about humor—"Hey, What's So Funny?"—for a nursing journal and reslanted it for a health magazine on the healing effects of humor in the workplace.

How-to: You name it, you can how-to it. Reviewing the magazine will tell you to what extent and depth the article must be taken to make it marketable. Do not discount the fact that some publications continually run novice material. For example, in a recent issue of *Bicycling* there was a beginning cyclist's guide to a healthy diet. Real basic stuff that they repeat in creative ways from time to time. Other sports magazines do this, too, as do health and women's magazines.

Life-style: This could mean gay/lesbian life-style or leisure/retirement life-style. Again, know the publication to which you are submitting.

Opinion and personal experience: These are the "Why We Should Have Gun Control" and "I Climbed El Capitan Blindfolded" pieces.

Romance: Depending on the guidelines of the magazine, romance could be R-rated or acceptable for G audiences. Sending a raunchy or risqué piece to a family magazine will only get you a rejection slip.

Seasonal: Go beyond Christmas, Hanukkah, and Columbus Day and think of "seasonal" as the first breath of spring, the shooting star shows that happen each August, and the time when you sent your first (or last) off to college or kindergarten.

Travel: Look at the magazine closely and don't overlook that you may live in an area that is the perfect focus for a travel piece.

Regarding the genres publishers will buy, find examples of the publishers' books. Save time and money by doing some homework on exactly what the magazine or book publisher buys before you query.

1.13   Getting It for Free or for Next to Nothing

Before the advent of money, people bartered; so did the pioneers. And, by golly, smart writers do it, too. If you need something, whether it's illustrations for an article or the use of a piece of equipment, try to barter. Your ability to write a well-thought-out sentence is valuable.

A friend and talented writer just received a book contract. This is her first book and she asked me to edit the manuscript for content and glaring grammatical faux pas. She offered to pay, but for me she has something more valuable. She's probably the best dog obedience instructor on the face of the earth and holds weekly classes to get dog and owner ready for the American Kennel Club's obedience competition. We bartered. My dog and I will receive free classes for an entire year and she gets the benefit of my years of writing and selling, on call, anytime.

Local business people need brochures and advertorials. Your city's politicians need speeches written. Unless they're looking to be indicted, the city probably won't pave your driveway. However, since most local political officials have "real" jobs, you may have the mayor's company paint your house or get months worth of landscaping services. Need dental work? Suggest a newsletter for your dentist to send to all her patients.

You get the picture. The possibilities in your own backyard are endless when you barter your services.

1.14   Getting Other Good Stuff for Free

A few years ago I wrote a nostalgic food article for the Automobile Club of America's magazine, *Westways*. "A Salute to the Kernel" was beautifully illustrated with popcorn photos courtesy of the American Popcorn Institute. The charge for these photos? Zip.

Your library has listings of organizations that knock themselves out to get their names/products in publications. Manufacturing companies, I've found, are also most helpful when you mention their products in your copy. Yes, you must give credit, but no money should change hands (I make that clear right at the beginning.).

What do you say to get free stuff once you have the phone number of the company or organization? To the person who answers the phone: "Hello. My name is (please fill in your own) and I'm writing an article for *Better Homes and Gardens*. I need some information, illustrations or transparencies (which are like big colored slides) for my article. Would you please direct my call to the correct department? Who will I be speaking to?"

And when you reach the person who is responsible for publicity, again state your name (spell it, too), why you're calling, and what you want. "I will, of course, give credit to the Cornflake Flakers of America and return the transparencies along with a tear sheet." Thank the individual, and be as good as your word. Do what you say and you'll be able to contact the company for other free stuff when you do spin-off articles on a similar topic.

1.15 Newsletter Writers Take Note

Linda Abel, publisher of *The Medieval Chronicle,* a newsletter devoted to fans of medieval novels, says, "Offer published authors free advertisements for their books in exchange for writing an article for your newsletter. If you'd like them to write more than one article, give them a discount on advertising.

"Also, don't be hesitant to ask manufacturing companies, publishers, and even celebrities for something free. In my newsletter, I use book reviews. By asking the publishers to send galleys, everybody wins. My readers get sneak previews. I get good, timely copy. The authors get publicity to their targeted reader and the publisher gets free editorial coverage."

1.16   Dressing for Success

As you're getting ready for your next appointment to interview an expert, drop a manuscript off at a magazine or newspaper, or meet an editor or agent, take another look in your mirror. Would you hire that person strictly by the way he/she looks? Judging a book or person by the "cover" is unfair—every grown-up knows that. But we also know that life isn't always just. Therefore, regardless of what you wear in your office, make sure you have two or three professional outfits, simple or sophisticated, clean and neat. If you do not own a briefcase, buy a few inexpensive, sturdy envelopes to transport material and notes.

When you look professional, you act more professional and only your work is evaluated.

1.17   Adding a Special Touch to Your Work

For those who are aware of fashion, it's known that sometimes less equals perfection. It's those tiny touches: a solitaire diamond, a string of impeccable pearls, the ideal little black dress, and the sparkling evening bag.

In writing, those little touches shout that you are a professional and you should be considered as such.

Therefore, here are some do's and don't's:

Do triple-check everything for accuracy. WordPerfect makes perfect words, but can't recognize when "that" should be "hat."

Don't bind manuscripts in any fancy method. It's unnecessary and expensive to place the manuscript in a folder, like a high school report. If you have a fat manuscript, use a folding clip for the top.

Do give your manuscript style. Make it clean and neat and present it on time.

Don't duplicate your manuscript on fancy paper, but do use at least twenty-pound bond. Tear off tractor-feeder edges if you use continuous paper.

Do add extra touches. I personally like to use blue paper clips which match the color ink used to print my name and address on my stationery. A very successful self-promoting writer uses gold-colored paper clips. These additions are tasteful and catch an editor's eye.

1.18 Photo Included or Not?

While there are two schools of thought on this topic, most writers think if you're applying for a modeling job, you should include a photo. If you're seeking literary representation or wanting to seize the interest of an editor, don't send one, regardless of your beauty. It's your writing style they want to see—not your hairstyle.

1.19   A Never-Ending Source for Writing
Material and Experts to Interview

How would you like thousands of sensational ideas for magazine articles and be able to contact the experts who can give you insider tips? How would you like them for free? Try the Yellow Pages. Really.

If you want to do an article on cryogenic research and development, it's there. If you want to write on the silliest singing telegrams, you'll find info in the phone book. If you're ever in the need for an expert, the Yellow Pages can do the trick, too. Remember, people who are in a specific business are experts whether they are carpet layers or astrologers.

The Yellow Pages not only provide the topics that are of interest to consumers and the experts to interview, many also list local cultural events and places of interest. These local items are outstanding for the community newspaper or regional periodicals, and are wonderful topics for national publications, too. The Garlic Gala, Chili Contest, Bathtub Regatta, and Ice Fishing Fun Day could all supply a theme for an article you could sell to a dozen magazines. As they say, "Let your fingers do the walking."

1.20   The Entrepreneurial Writer

If your brother, aunt, or cousin-in-law is head of a publishing giant, you might have a chance to use your influence to get outstanding magazine writing assignments or plum book deals. But if you're like the rest of us, you must become an opportunist. Don't wait for opportunity to knock; dash out and grab it in the street.

In today's careful economic climate, you must make your own name known and carve your own niche. If a topic is hot, run with it. If you see an opportunity, snatch it. This includes self-publishing your book (if you have the funds and energy to promote it), writing newsletters about specific careers or causes, and ghostwriting. Be willing to push your advantage with words to get business.

1.21 Insuring That Your Query Letter Gets Through

Should you need to know the how-to's of queries, check out some of the books mentioned in the "Recommended Reading" list at the end of this book. Here are some tips to make sure that the query you've slaved over gets into the right editor's hands:

• Look at the masthead of the magazine (that's where all the editors and staff are listed; usually found in the first few pages). If you're writing a query to one of the departments, send your letter to the editor who handles that field. Sending the query to the editor-in-chief, production manager, or managing editor may insure it gets slowed or lost in the shuffle.

• Don't be cheap. Get the address from *Literary*

Market Place, The Writer's Handbook, or *Writers Digest* and call for the correct editor's name, unless you've read a recent entry in a writer's magazine. With many magazines, the cliché that begins "here today" was written with editors in mind.

• While you're on the phone, double-check the address and ask for the zip-plus-four code to speed delivery.

• If you've talked on the phone with the editor about your topic, you might want to write "Query Requested" on the outside of the envelope.

• Always enclose an SASE if you want a response. Also make sure your phone number is on the stationery you use. Often editors are as short on time as they are on clerical staff and prefer to contact writers about a specific idea or an off-shoot of your query. If your phone number isn't listed the work will go to another writer.

• And should an editor like your query, but want to suggest that you send another one on a different topic, do so as soon as possible. Pat yourself on the back. You've just gotten an incredible lead and possibly regular writing work.

1.22   The One-a-Day Success Plan

This sounds exceedingly simple but the results are phenomenal. To be a magazine writer who regularly sells his or her work, all you have to do is send out query letters.

A number of years ago I vowed to send out at least one query letter a day—this was before I bought my first word processing system, too. Sure, I got rejections; but I also got work.

The trick is to send queries every single day . . . or one for every day of the week (i.e. write seven on Monday and skate for the next six days while writing assigned articles).

1.23 Making a Mint with Smaller Publications

As a veteran writer you know that selling to *Playboy, Good Housekeeping,* or *National Geographic* will boost your reported income quite nicely. However, the odds of doing so are probably about as long as winning big in Las Vegas. As a seasoned pro who might get a little frustrated with those chances, you should give smaller magazines a third look.

Sure they have smaller circulation and fee schedules, but they are excellent markets for savvy writers because they will appreciate you, provide assignments, and give you the opportunity to resell your material to non-competing magazines. One article for a big periodical could bring in $2,000, but that might include lots of rewrites. However, if you wrote, for example, an article on exotic vegetables, you could possibly sell it to *Florida Living* (for $200) and other regional magazines (for a total of over $1,000). Reslant it and sell it to *Trailer Life* (for $500). Rewrite it again, selling it to *Women's Circle* (for

$125) and *Vim & Vigor* (for $450). And this just begins the possibilities.

Suddenly that simple but well-written little piece is worth as much as writing for one of the persnickety magazines and you'll probably get more assignments and better money with the next assignments, too.

1.24 Turning Local Stories into National News with National Scope

As you read in "A Never-ending Source for Writing Material and Experts to Interview" above, there's material for entertaining and marketable articles everywhere. Don't ever swallow the concept that just because you live in the suburbs nothing of national significance ever goes on there. It's simply not so.

Let's say you are one of the volunteers who is improving the quality of housing for low-income families. Every Saturday you and fifty other church members spend twelve hours cleaning, painting, and rebuilding practically uninhabitable homes in your town or city. What a heart-warming plethora of material! There's plenty for an article on volunteerism, citizens reaching out to help improve living standards, team spirit (and Christian fellowship) alive and well in the nineties, and (perhaps even) the disgrace of local welfare offices that are unable to assist those who are practically destitute. These are just a few possibilities. Now, tie your concept into a national movement focused on the main theme, interview other groups from Butte to Savannah, and you've got national news that will sell.

The notion is simple. Find a topic that is important in your town and research how this idea applies to America. See what else has been published on this topic or other similar topics. Then get back to your computer and get cracking. If you think the issue is timely and saleable, then somebody, somewhere is thinking the same thought. Get your query on an editor's desk before your competition realizes that fact.

Lots of excellent books have come from the nuggets mined in the magazine writing process. Look further than a magazine. Why not propose a book on volunteering, using this same technique? The example above might be called *Helping Hands*. When the proposal is submitted to publishers, you have a credible clip to show that the public wants to read about this topic.

1.25   Giving It Away Free. Knowing When It Makes Sense

There are times when it makes sense to write for free, instead of taking a ridiculously small amount of money. It's a fact of life that many of us are underpaid as it is, and when a writer accepts an absurd fee, it is a disservice to us all.

Soap boxes aside, what's a self-respecting writer to do when offered slave wages? Consider negotiating, bartering, or simply making a wonderful gesture and doing a *small* amount of writing work for free.

Not too long ago a firm I wrote for asked me to update some previously written material for the corporate newsletter, since the technology had changed. I had been paid for the previous work, but they'd never used it. During the same phone call, their marketing department had also asked me to write three feature articles for future newsletters.

I knew it would take about an hour to revise the articles—they were on disk. I chose to do the revision for free (making it clear this was a one-time-only deal). Of course, I received my usual rate for the other articles.

Other instances in which you might work for free are when a beginner needs a helping hand (editing, critiquing, writing a query or proposal) or when a cause screams out for a great writer. Yes, this sounds like bad business advice, but by doing work for free, you keep your self-respect. Writing for a pittance, you don't.

1.26   Pen Names. Who Needs 'em?

Why would a writer use a pen name? Often it's done to conceal his or her identity for one reason or another; sometimes it's done to make the article more appealing.

I was asked to select a pen name when writing (on a regular basis) for a fitness magazine. The editor said he'd be uncomfortable having in the June issue three articles plus a regular column by Eva Shaw, yet he wanted to use all four. So for a while I was Tanya Tanaka, William Nash, and Evan McCall.

If you choose to use a pen name, for whatever purpose, be sure to let the editor know. (I would have had trouble cashing William Nash's check!) If you will always be writing under an alias, you may have to file a fictitious name statement with your city and advertise in the newspaper, before your bank will honor those checks.

1.27   What Agents Do and Don't Do

Literary agents represent you in the publishing world. They negotiate contracts, clarify publishing issues on your behalf, smooth ruffled feathers, referee when necessary, and generally look out for your best interests. Obviously when you make money and sell lots of books, and have lots of contracts, they make more money.

Literary agents are marketing people. Their job is to sell your talent with the written word. They are not, in most cases, editors or writers. Don't expect your agent to tell you specifically what needs to be rewritten in your book. More often than not, they'll simply tell you that your proposal or idea isn't right for their agency.

The secret to finding an agent you can work with is really subjective. Some writers want aggressive agents who will shake fists, slam doors, and demand the moon. Other writers want the low-key or scholarly types. Personally, I have to be represented by someone who is assertive and ethical, with a good sense of humor and with whom I can feel comfortable chatting over a cup of coffee. Fortunately, there are agents like this in the industry.

However, like the short-order cook knows, sometimes you have to throw out the first pancake that comes from the grill. The same goes with agents. Don't be stumped if the first agent you select isn't the right one. The second one could be Ms. or Mr. Right.

1.28   How an Agent Evaluates a Client and a Book Deal

Literary agent Bert Holtje, of James Peter Associates, Inc., points out that the book "deal" is more than an advance.

"Recently, I considered taking on a new client, an author with seven rather successful books to his credit. His previous agent was retiring and had given him the names of several agents he felt might be appropriate. The author called me and we did the dance authors and agents do when they first talk. I talked of my successes and he talked of his.

"Quickly, the subject became money. The author's advances had gone from ordinary to quite good. And his royalties had shown the same progression. Then he said, 'I have decided that I cannot do a book anymore for less than a *blah blah* advance.' The figure was not unreasonable. But his view of the publishing process was. I tried to point out that there are many other elements in the equation. Royalty percentages and jumps. Sub-rights splits. Promotion. He said flat out that he wouldn't do another book for a lesser advance, regardless of other terms. I said thanks, but no thanks.

"Every book has its own profit and loss picture. And, sure, a publisher is going to be more flexible with an author with a good track record, but no publisher is going to offer advance money that cannot be earned out.

"Negotiate for as much money as you can, but remember that advance money doesn't go up automatically with each succeeding book the way salaries often increase when you move from one job to a better one. Look at the total picture. What else is the publisher putting on the table? Will the publisher commit to an advertising budget? How about a tour?

"An author I represent is accustomed to low-six-figure advances. Recently, he took a book for less than $10,000. But . . . we both knew that this was a book that would become a backlist title and would earn him far in excess of the higher advances he had formerly received."

Bert Holtje's best trade secret: "Negotiate for the best advance you can get, but don't wear blinders when you do it."

1.29 Unstick the Agent/Editor Waiting Game

M. Sue Lasbury, San Diego literary agent, points out, "Often writers feel it's immoral to send query letters to more than one agent or editor at a time. This is an antiquated method of doing business." She compares this tactic to putting in an application for employment to only one company then waiting to see if, by chance, they have an opening and if they'll consider hiring.

"Do it professionally, but give the agent/editor a deadline to review your material and get back to you. I believe that an agent should be able to review a query and/or a proposal within three weeks. Be sure to include an SASE or postcard. If you still do not hear after that time, call.

"I think some agents keep writers in bondage, usurping the writer's power. Do not relinquish your power when you are marketing a book proposal. This is your career."

SECTION
2

The Buck Stops Here

If you're looking for retirement information for writers or how to write and live on five dollars a day, this section isn't for you. Other great books have tips on budgeting, retirement, and financial planning. Visit your bookstore or library. However, should you want to know how to keep more of what you make, you're in the right place.

The dream of most writers is to make more money. Most of us think that will happen through creative, intelligent hard work. Those who have been in the writing game for a while understand that this concept is only part of the puzzle. Because regardless of how much money you make, it's what you keep that counts. Stretching those bucks is what makes the difference in your income. That's what we'll focus on in this section.

2.1 Saving on Office Equipment and Software

Barter, buy on sale, shop the classified ads, and see what you can trade to save money on office equipment and software.

Second-hand stores often have wonderful old office furniture, if you're into that sturdy-wood look. Paint or polish can do miracles. Companies with rooms full of great furniture go bankrupt and have auctions to pay off the creditors. They sometimes have spectacular office furniture and computer equipment for just a fraction of the original cost. Other writers update the stuff in their offices and would like to sell what they had. You can always set up your writing space on a table or a flat wooden door balanced between two small filing cabinets. The point here is, you have to shop around and ask.

If you're buying new office equipment, find out the cost of delivery. Sometimes you can buy a little extra (which you really need) and barter to have the furniture delivered free. Compare that cost with other stores, too. Keep all receipts; even the delivery is a legitimate business expense.

Before buying software, try the program out at the store or at a friend's. Not too long ago, a writing program was advertised that would put an end to awkward sentences and make every sentence grammatically perfect. Do you remember it? What a temptation. I excitedly tried it, knowing I'd love it, but it didn't love my writing style. If I had chosen to use it, I would have spent hours telling my monitor that I preferred the way I'd originally written a manuscript, or I would have turned out a stuffy piece, without spark or sizzle. Perhaps for someone who writes only textbooks or technical manuals, it would be a good investment. For me, it would have been a nightmare.

When buying software, make sure the software store will give your money back if the software 1) doesn't work with your setup or 2) proves too simple or difficult for your application. Most stores will refund your money, but you must ask (and get the name of the clerk who tells you that's so).

2.2 Special Note on Software Savings or Software Nightmares

"Hey, you there. Wanna' copy of this great new program? A writer like you should save some money. Half the original price and it's yours."

Well-meaning friends, computer hackers, and a slew of others are out there to tempt you. *However,* buying pirated copies of software is not only illegal, it's potentially fatal considering the various viruses lurking in computer programs these days. Sure you can save $100 or more, but if your computer crashes or munches your book or articles because of a virus, you'll be in big trouble. And buying a pirated copy is almost like an editor using your latest manuscript without paying you a cent. It's stealing, pure and simple.

When you buy an original copy, you get the manuals, store assistance, and most likely an 800 telephone number for technical support with a knowledgeable person at the software company. For those of us who are only marginally computer literate, that's well worth the cost.

2.3 Saving Money on Continuous Computer Paper

Use twenty-pound paper to print a final manuscript. Use sixteen pound for rough drafts of manuscripts. Remember: Paper has two sides. If a box of paper cost you twenty dollars and you can use both sides for drafts, you've saved ten dollars plus a trip to the stationery store. (See "Save Money by Being an Environmentally Friendly Writer" below for more tips.)

2.4 Save Money by Being an Environmentally Friendly Writer

Immortalizing your words is simpler than you think, says Cory J Meacham, assistant editor with *San Diego Writers Monthly,* who explains what every environmentally friendly writer should know: The pages you throw in the trash guarantee that your words will live on and on—in a stagnant landfill. Submit those scrap pages to your local recycler, however, and your mistakes become contributions.

Here are thirteen equally simple and effective ways to avoid wasteful work habits common to the writing trade. None detract from your professional image. Several help you save time and money.

• Write, type, or print on recycled paper. Everything from spiral-bound note pads to tractor-feed white bond is available.

• Use unbleached paper for rough drafts and file copies. Considerable amounts of energy, water, and harsh chemicals are needed to make paper white.

• Remember that every piece of paper has two sides. The backs of used sheets are perfect for rough drafts and note taking. Conserving one sheet of paper does more for the environment than recycling two.

• Bring your own recycled paper to the copy shop, or go to a shop that provides it. If you own a copier, fill it with recycled paper.

• Purchase writing accessories made of recycled or biodegradable materials. Ecologically sensible envelopes, address labels, file folders, push pins, adhesive tape, and removable adhesive notes are available.

• Write with wooden pencils rather than pens or pencils made of plastic. If you must use plastic writing tools, use refillable ones.

• Reink typewriter and printer ribbons, and refill the tone cartridges used in laser printers and copy machines.

• Turn off equipment that's not in use. The average typewriter, computer, printer, or copier left idling for a year at forty hours per week will waste the equivalent of a barrel of oil. Batch the jobs to be done and fire up each machine individually.

• Don't mail something you can FAX, and don't FAX when you can phone. Important note: Environmental awareness is NOT a valid reason to FAX or phone your queries to editors who don't okay such methods.

• FAX responsibly. Fill your machine with recycled paper, and substitute removable adhesive transmittal notes for full-size cover sheets. Be aware that thermal FAX paper (the thin, shiny stuff that comes in rolls) is not widely accepted for recycling even though it is now being made from recycled material; plain paper FAX machines, although more expensive than thermal machines, can be stocked with inexpensive sheets that are both recycled and recyclable. Installing a modem and a FAX board in your computer eliminates the need to use paper at all when transmitting, and allows you to print selectively when receiving.

• Submit work electronically. Many publishers now accept submissions on disk or via modem. Inquire first.

• Begin recycling. Talk with recyclers in your area. You may need to separate the typical paper discards of writing into three types: white bond (doesn't need to be bleached as heavily and therefore brings a better price at commercial recycling centers); coated (glossy magazines mainly, but includes anything slick with heavy printing); and everything else. All three types are to be separated from newspaper.

Cory's final tip: Recycle this information and share it with other writers.

(The timely piece first appeared in *Writer's Digest*, May 1992.)

2.5 A P.S. to the Environmentally Friendly Writer

As a postscript, here are some other recycling tips to consider:

- Ask the folks at your quick print store to make pads of their scrap paper. If it bothers you to write notes on the "clean" side, type or write "Recycling Makes Sense" across the used side of the paper to explain to anyone who sees the recycled paper.
- Get two uses from tractor-fed computer paper. Do not separate sheets when doing rough drafts. On your next rough draft, feed it through with the clean side up.
- Often you can recycle a letter by writing your response on the bottom. Make a note of what transpired on your original copy or on the computer copy stored on your hard disk.
- Share recycling responsibilities. After separating paper, as Cory suggested above, take turns with other writers to deliver the paper to the center. You may only need to go to the center once every three or four months.
- Remember: Junk mail is recyclable, as is the carton in which your computer ribbon is purchased.
- Recycle folders by placing new adhesive labels over previous ones, then turning the folder inside out for a whole new-looking folder, with many more lives.

37

• If you do a lot of taped interviewing, use the envelopes that junk mail comes in to store the tapes. Staple them safely shut. The envelopes give you room to make notes, add the date of the interview, etc.

2.6 Sometimes Discount Doesn't Mean Less Expensive

Do you know that you could actually be wasting money by buying your supplies at the big discount warehouse?

Ask the local stationery shop for a business-owner's discount on supplies. You should be entitled to a discount of at least ten percent; I get a fifteen percent discount and another writer who buys a whole lot more gets twenty percent off. The stationery store may actually be as inexpensive as the warehouse discount store.

You'll probably save even more when you consider the time and gasoline conserved (not to mention reducing a few pollutants in the environment). You'll also avoid the temptation of buying things you don't have on your list.

You can order what you need, impossible at the discount warehouse, and that means you won't have to shop around in another store.

2.7 Save Money When Buying Books Directly from a Publisher

Who doesn't love a bargain? Save from five-to-twenty percent when buying books from a publisher or self-published author by asking if there are any slightly damaged copies available for sale. As you know the bookstores and book distributors like Baker and Taylor will not sell slightly damaged books. Sometimes what you save can be at least half the price of a book you need and want.

2.8   Mail It Right

An accurate postage scale for in-office measurements could save money, every day. It will keep you from pasting too much postage on that envelope. Weigh all envelopes.

You can call the post office and ask how much postage should be affixed to a specific mailing, such as for foreign airmail when you know exactly how much the envelope weighs.

Obtain a chart of postal fees and keep a supply of various stamp denominations on hand.

Using a postal substation, sometimes located in stationery stores, can save you time. They're usually not crowded, and do handle express mail delivery, but often do not handle the mailing of foreign packages.

For tax purposes, get a receipt every time you use a postal service. If you buy stamps from a machine, write the amount paid, date, and location on a slip of paper. Place it in the appropriate bookkeeping file or envelope for a tax-time deduction.

2.9   Saving Money on Batteries

Do you use a tape recorder to interview? Use rechargeable batteries. You'll save time and money, and help the environment, too.

2.10   Speaking of Tape Recorders

If you use a hand-held, microcassette tape recorder, give it two lives (1) for interviewing and (2) for making notes such as when you're driving and stuck in traffic.

Always triple-check that the tape recorder is functioning before doing an interview. It's a waste of time (and makes you seem less than professional) if you have to admit to the subject of your article that you must reinterview him or her since the tape recorder didn't work correctly.

And before you begin interviewing over the telephone, always let the person you're going to talk with know that you've turned on the tape. "I'm going to tape this interview, Ms. Jones, and I've turned on the machine. Is that okay?" Wait for the response, then begin. Here in California, that's the law. Check in your own state.

For about $60, you can buy a telephone answering machine with a two-way record feature so that, at the push of a button, you can use it as an answering machine when you're unavailable, or you can record important phone conversations (alerting the caller of what you're doing).

2.11   Give Your FAX a Dual Role

A FAX machine is great not only for the obvious reasons, but because it can double as a copier. No, the copies won't be as sharp as a personal copier, yet sometimes you just need a copy, any kind of copy. With a small copy machine, to get really clear copies or to do a bunch of them, you'll want to go to a copy shop.

2.12   Have Your "Own" FAX Without Paying a Penny for the Machine

If you are a regular customer at a stationery store or copy shop, ask the business's permission to use their FAX number on your correspondence. Sure you'll have to pay when they receive a FAX for you, but if you don't use this service often, it's extremely economical.

2.13   Transcribing Ease

A cassette tape transcriber with a foot-pedal control (so you can transcribe in a flash the tapes you make with your tape recorder) will cut time in thirds.

Before you record an interview, always set the counter on your tape recorder to zero. Using the numbers on the recorder, make notes when the subject of the interview says something especially important. You can skim right back to the pertinent spot(s) without listening to the entire tape.

2.14 A Telephone Headset Could Be Like Having Two Pairs of Hands

An "operator, can-I-help-you-please?" telephone head-set will set your hands free to use the keyboard during phone interviews or to take notes in longhand. And when you're put on hold, you will have the opportunity to do something more valuable than drum your fingers on the desk. It's far more comfortable than cradling the receiver in the crook of your neck.

2.15 Save Money with Illustrations

Depending on what you're writing you may need illus-trations, but sometimes it's a waste of money to hire an illustrator before the book or article is accepted.

Professional illustrator Pam Posey, who draws "Thomas the Tank Engine" and has worked on books for Harcourt Brace and Jovanovich, Crown Publishers, Random House, and Thomas Nelson Publishers, explains, "Before you go to the expense of hiring an illustrator, find out what type of illustrations are expected, are they necessary for the sale of the project and who does the editor want to do them?

"I've found with children's books, especially, many writers think that they must send finished art work along with the manuscript. This could be a major expense that is unnecessary. Often, manuscripts are sold without illustrations with the writer doing a rough sketch of the art for each caption. The publisher uses a staff artist or other freelancer for the work."

2.16   Stretching Your Supply Budget

• Whenever possible buy a larger, less costly quantity of supplies, splitting the supplies with other writers. For example, if I buy a dozen felt-tipped pens at the stationery store, the price is only sixty cents each. If I buy them individually, I spend a buck. Knowing I can use the pens, the $4.80 savings is well worth it. Again, ask for quantity discounts—you'll probably get them.

• Share an expensive reference book with another writer, if appropriate.

• Sell equipment or supplies that you are not using. That extra desk and chair that are gathering dust could be turned into cash, thus allowing you to buy more business cards or treat yourself to a conference. A writer I know recently bought a new computer system which used the $3\frac{1}{2}''$ disks. She sold two unopened boxes of $5\frac{1}{4}''$ disks to a journalist friend. The disks were valuable to the other writer, especially at a savings.

• If you can't sell equipment or books, or prefer not to, donate them to your favorite charity or a school. Get a receipt and check with your accountant. This should be a deduction.

2.17   Save Money When You Travel

If you ever go out of town on business, you need these tips on saving money when traveling. *Hour Power* by John W. Lee and Milt Pierce (Dow Jones–Irwin Publishers, 1980) has some excellent tips on saving time for every business person, and here are two especially pertinent to writers.

The authors recommend the following: "The cardinal rule for avoiding rip-offs when traveling is NEVER TELL ANYONE YOU ARE NEW IN TOWN. Even if you go to Atlanta with a Brooklyn accent, tell people you come down this way all the time. The business traveler who runs around telling salesmen and cabdrivers how little they know about this city are the easiest marks in the world. They wind up traveling five miles to get across a two-mile town. They pay the highest prices possible for second-class goods. They have set themselves up to lose money. So under any circumstances, pretend you know something about where you are.

"The second rule is IF YOU FEEL YOU ARE BEING RIPPED-OFF, SAY SO. There is no way to defend your rights and protect yourself unless you speak up. Be sure the people you suspect of thievery know you are ready and willing to take bold action against them. If you keep your complaints to yourself, you will never get results."

2.18 Getting Photos for a Better Price. You Could Save at Least $4.50 on Each Photo

Some writers keep a press kit available to promote themselves and their books. Some writers pay a pretty penny for black-and-white glossy photos to include in the press kit. Don't do it. Have the original photo professionally taken by a pro who knows make-up and how to make you look sharp, then shop around for photographic duplication services. Some places offer 5″ × 7″ photos for as low as ten-to-fifty cents each; your hometown photo studio may charge you five dollars each.

2.19 Save Money by Having the Correct Writing Tools

If you're still plunking out manuscripts on an antique Smith-Corona, a sincere bravo. However, unless you're addicted to finger torture, consider the time and energy you'll save by switching to a computerized word processing system. Sure it'll cost some money—anywhere between one thousand and four thousand dollars, depending on your taste for micro-chips—but using a computer system as opposed even to an electronic typewriter with memory can cut the grind work of producing clean manuscripts by as much as two thirds. Translate that into productive time to sell more writing. You can have the system paid for within a month.

As you shop for a new system or to upgrade what you have, ask about trade-ins, sales, and what will be given as an incentive to buy (e.g. various software packages). Sell your old typewriter or donate it to a charity.

If you are not computer literate, take one of those computer classes that are only one day long—even before you select your new system—to have an understanding of what you can expect. Once your system arrives in your office, you may want to hire a computer whiz to teach you some specific tricks to cut your grind time even lower.

2.20   Make More Money Selling Foreign and Reprints

The *International Literary Market Place* (found in most libraries) is an excellent source for magazines which would love to buy articles that have been published in the United States. Sure you'll have to invest some time at the library and money for stamps, but the return can be a gold mine.

First make some crisp photocopies of the article, listing where and when the article was first printed. Next make a list of the foreign publications that might buy this type of material. And finally, send a cover letter, the article, and a self-addressed envelope to the foreign publication.

I just sold another article I originally wrote in 1988 to a Tokyo-based magazine for Japanese business people. This makes three sales to various foreign publications for the same piece. The article, "Do Mondays Make You Sick?" is scheduled for publication shortly, and I've already received payment of about one hundred dollars with a check drawn on a California-based bank.

Once an article has been printed, even if you've sold all rights, ask for your copyrights back. You may have to wait a few months, but normally they will be returned to you if you ask. Then do not delay. Resell that article.

For more information and marketable tips on reselling articles, you may want to review my book *Writing and Selling Magazine Articles,* also in the Paragon House Writer's Series.

2.21 Dust Off Your Camera and Make More Money

I am not an Ansel Adams, or even worthy of holding his camera. However, I have sold a number of photos that accompanied articles. These were not travel articles, although I've sold quite a few of those, too. The photos here were to be included with articles on fitness walking (showing my husband with a group out stretching their legs), household fire safety (showing my husband holding a fire extinguisher), and the benefits of redwood decking (me and my dog sedately sitting on the wooden deck— the time-delay function was used).

You can make more money this way, too. Photos help sell articles. With an investment of four dollars for film, you can easily make an additional twenty-five to one hundred dollars or more on an article.

If you don't know a lens cap from a distributor cap, you

can still make some extra money, but first take a class in photography at your local community college. There are also some fine how-to books at your library or bookstore. Borrow a camera if you don't own one—at least at first. Sometimes camera shops have excellent used cameras for a fraction of the original price and will even give you a few lessons (if you ask).

If you're just an okay photographer, I sincerely recommend the excellent videos produced by Kodak. Watch them two and three times, then practice exactly what is explained on the films. They work.

As you query, explain that color slides will accompany the article. Magazines do not normally work from colored photos as they don't reproduce as well as slides. If the magazine uses only black-and-white photos, you can (most of the time) still send in color slides, unless the guidelines specifically ask for black-and-white photos. Check the guidelines or with the editor as to what they want before you buy film.

To lure an editor into making an assignment, you may want to send along a tantalizing photo or duplicate slide with the query. For example, if you're writing an article on wooden planters built from scrap lumber, build a planter, take some shots, and include them with your query. Put some saucy petunias in the pot or sit a cat (or a kid) next to the planter for extra appeal.

When having film developed, ask for a proof or contact sheet. What you'll get are tiny (approximately 3/4-inch square) exposures of each photo. Use a magnifying glass to see the results, then select the ones that look best. The owner of the camera shop should be able to help you decide which are the sharpest of the batch. A proof sheet costs far less than having the entire roll of film developed into pictures you may or may not be able to use.

Don't be put off because only three out of the thirty-six exposures turn out to be acceptable. Remember, professional photographers take rolls to get that perfect photo.

2.22 Get a Photo Release

If you use people in your shots, it's always good business practice to get photo releases from these folks when taking the pictures. A photo release can be a simple typed form stating the person's name and the fact that you have paid this individual a certain amount for modeling (or that no money is expected for this service). Have the form signed and dated.

Some magazines and publishers will want you to send photo releases along with the photos.

2.23 Cutting Down the Cost of a Call

• *Always,* if at all possible, call when you get the least expensive rates. Those of us who live on the West Coast can call the East at a genuine discount and catch our editors and publisher before lunch by calling before 8:00 A.M. If you live in the East, call the Coast after five. Live in Denver, Topeka, or White Horse? Check the front of your phone book for time-zone info before you let your fingers get close to the telephone.

• Jot down notes as to exactly what you want to ask or discuss before you use the telephone, even on long-distance calls in your county or state.

• Talk to your phone system representative about getting one of the bonus calling options or other discounts that are available.

• When someone is calling you long-distance, respect their time and budget by staying on the topic and limiting the time.

• If you're unable to reach the person you're calling, leave a message that includes exactly who you are, time and day you've called, the subject of your call, and a convenient time when you can be called back. Otherwise you could end up playing telephone tag.

2.24 Save Time—Don't Let Writer's Block Get to You

Is writer's block a hoax perpetuated by those hounding the pages of a dictionary for just the right word? Is it an excuse for those who talk about writing . . . and only talk? Is it a creative recess necessary to produce ingenious thoughts?

Basically, it's a major waste of time, which in any writer's language spells a major waste of earning potential. And whether it's real or imaginary (and I think it's the latter), the best way to deal with writer's block is to ignore it. Those who make their living writing and those who are addicted to the written word hardly ever await bolts of inspiration. Even if the words don't come easily, they'll come.

The trick to overcoming brain slow-down is to continue to write. You can always go back and edit. Just get it down. As discussed in one of my other books, *Ghostwriting: How to Get into the Business* (also for the Paragon House Writer's Series, 1991), there are times when the right words simply don't come. This happens, usually, when you're dealing with other stressors in life—in addition to writing.

So if words don't come, get out of the office or your home for an hour, take a walk or get some exercise, then get back to work on that project or another one on which you are working. If that doesn't work, begin on a different article or book, or go back to your previously published articles. Organize them, make copies, and send them out for reprint sales.

We all have "those days" when nothing goes smoothly, but that has nothing to do with writer's block. If you are still unable to put ten words together and sound reasonably intelligent, though, here's a list of alternatives.

- Go to the library for research and learn how to use the various computer search programs available at most large libraries.
- Reread or retype material you've already written to improve it.
- Play with your computer until you can do twice as

much as you can now. Learn how to do what the program tells you it can do such as graphics, spreadsheets, macros, etc.

• Write letters, including thank-you notes to editors, friends, networking contacts.

• Contact new or perspective magazines or publishers. Locate a bookstore that sells some of the writer magazines other than *Writer's Digest* and *The Writer*. Buy some copies and become reinspired.

• Make lists of what's needed to complete this project. Then start at the top and go straight through the list.

• Up-date your query file.

• Submit your queries and consider offering your own photos to accompany the articles.

• Organize your office and materials.

• Have a quick chat with another writer to discuss your current problem. Get his or her input.

• Do anything that helps your writing, from reviewing a manual on grammar to reading books on dialogue and characterization.

• Keep in mind that good nonfiction must be as captivating as fiction to entice today's reader.

2.25   Save Hundreds of Dollars with Magazine Subscriptions

You can save a bundle of money if you share magazine subscriptions with other writers. You can do it by splitting the initial costs or by having each member of the group subscribe to a different magazine.

To make this system work, the ground rules must be defined and everyone involved needs to know what is expected. This is how we do it. Three of my writing friends and I have all, at one time or another, wanted to subscribe to *Publishers Weekly*. At nearly $120 a year, it's somewhat pricey. However, by splitting the cost four ways, it's reasonable. (We also share subscriptions to other writer's magazines.) When the magazine arrives at Linda's office, she attaches a routing slip to the cover (the slip is like those used in an office). She has three days to read the magazine, then it's passed on at the same speed until everyone has seen the copy. No one is allowed to tear anything out (we make photocopies of articles) until it's made its rounds. Should one of us want the magazine when it's finished circulating, we indicate that next to our name on the routing slip. If no one wants the magazine, it's donated to the library, a writing class, or tossed into the recycling bin—whatever is appropriate.

How much money can be saved? With *PW* alone, we've each saved over ninety dollars this year.

This can work with other magazines and newsletters, as well. If you and another writer both query women's, sports, or travel publications, start sharing those subscriptions. When it's only two of you, fold under the top corner of the cover if you want the magazine back after your friend has reviewed it. With no corner turned under, your friend need not return it.

2.26   Saving Money When Using Copy
Machines

When you have a few spare minutes, call a few copy shops to compare pricing on copies. Locally, copies range from fifteen cents each (at the machine within the post office) to two cents each (with a coupon from a major chain copy store).

And when making copies, if you don't get a receipt, write the amount of money spent, the date, and the reasons for the copies on a piece of paper (or keep a log). This should be a legitimate tax deduction.

2.27   Saving Money on Taxis and
Other Related Expenses

Always ask for receipts for parking and taxis. Sometimes that doesn't work—we both know it. Let's say you're madly attempting to make a train at Penn Station and you only remember you should have gotten a receipt from the taxi driver as you're on the Metroliner heading back to Washington, D.C. It's okay. Write the amount, the service, and the date on a piece of paper and include this in your tax file.

This is good advice for other related expenses, but again, check with your tax planner for the latest information.

2.28 A Telephone Log Could Save You Money

Every writer should keep a log of telephone calls. The log quickly lets you see which calls on your monthly bill are business deductions, and when writing for magazines, corporate clients, or some publishers you may need the info for reimbursements.

You can buy a log at the stationery store (for about eight dollars); however, for the time it takes to set up a list on your computer (just the cost of your time) or draw lines in a spiral binder, you can save at least seven dollars.

Here's what a telephone log looks like:

Date	Phone Number	Who Was Called	Who Will Be Charged
5/6	(619) 555-1212	K. Jones	*Great Living Magazine*
5/7	(212) 555-1212	L. Smith	*Horse Digest*
5/7	(302) 555-1212	J. Adams	*Industrial News*

2.29 Keep Your Records Straight and Save Money with a Mileage Log

When you're on assignment for a magazine, you'll often have mileage reimbursed. Keep a mileage log in your car for that purpose and perhaps your tax records, too. You are probably driving more business miles than you think.

You can buy official mileage logs at most stationery stores or simply keep a tiny, spiral bound tablet in your glove compartment. Keeping mileage is a habit that could save you considerable money.

SECTION
3

*Hour Power—Save Time,
Increase Productivity*

One of the tips that may not seem to be a sensible addition to this section is to take time for yourself. An hour of tennis or nine holes of golf, a trip with the kids to the zoo, a chat with a friend during lunchtime all work wonders to keep your mind sharp and body refreshed.

Staying healthy, eating a smart diet, and exercising will also give you the stamina you need to save time and increase productivity. If you do no other form of fitness, take a walk every day. As you're walking, boost your ego with affirmations, think through a knotty plot line, or mentally organize your workday.

Self-employed writers need vacations and weekends off, an afternoon at the beach, a trip to the shopping mall, and a bag of popcorn while sitting at the ball park. This down time is necessary, just like recess was when we were in elementary school.

3.1 Take a Short Walk Right Now

Reread the introduction above, if necessary, and then get out of the office for only five minutes. Straighten your posture, breathe deeply, swing your arms, and walk around the garden, up and down a flight of stairs, or to the end of the block and back. Repeat this anytime you need to clear your mind.

If you're absolutely, positively not the type to walk, stretching is great to get the brain cells functioning again, too.

3.2 Does Writing Have to Be Done in Solitude?

Nancy S. Grant, author of *Old Glory: A History and Celebration* from Random House says writers can write anywhere and anytime. Don't allow the solitude factor to stymie your work.

"Experienced writers know that the inspiration to put the words in the right order can come anywhere and anyplace, be it while driving the car, standing in line at the grocery, even watching a Braves' game. The lonely part can occur when you're sitting in front of the typewriter unable to remember just what it was that seemed so profound yesterday afternoon.

"When the words are flowing effortlessly that solitude disappears as we create the illusion of speaking directly

57

to our intended readers. But oh, how miserable, how forsaken we feel when verbs steadfastly refuse to link up with nouns!"

3.3 Postal Prompts

When time is of the essence (and you don't have the reason or resources for an express delivery service), drive to your city's central post office. By doing so, you'll typically speed your letter or package on its way by a full day. Be aware that central post offices sometimes have windows open for after-hours business.

Memorize the pick-up times at your local mail boxes and post office, then adjust your drop-off schedule accordingly. No need to have your outgoing mail sit idle for hours or maybe days on end.

3.4 Save Time with Replies—Include the Zip-plus-four

Call the post office and ask for your zip-plus-four extension. Include it on all SASEs. You can cut a full day off the return time of mail.

For those who use a post office box, make note: A box often has a different zip code than your town.

3.5 Tick, Tock, You're in Charge of the Clock. How to Find Time to Write

How do you feel about those folks who only use the good china once a year, keep the diamonds in a safety-deposit box, and say that "someday" they'll write a book or magazine article? Personally, I love them, because their existence means there's less competition for my writing.

Don't allow yourself to fall into this category of "some-dayers" because nine out of ten never make it.

If you are determined to be a published writer (or have more of your writing published) and you can afford to, quit your day job. However, keep in mind that *all* of the published writers I know, including myself, have other "jobs." In addition to writing books and articles under my byline, I ghostwrite for clients and read and evaluate manuscripts for a literary agency. I also lecture at conferences, colleges, and universities. Another writer I know works full-time as an interior decorator and writes on weekends and at night. A third is a public information officer and writes before she leaves for work in the morning.

Writing is the perfect career to do sometimes, part-time, or full-time. If teachers can do it in the summertime, police officers can do it when not on shift, and moms can do it when the kids are in school, you can do it, too.

Here's how: Think about or write down what you do on a typical work day, then examine the ways you could be more effective or efficient so you have time to write. For example, if you get up at six in the morning and spend an hour reading the paper or watching "Good Morning, Milwaukee," this could be the perfect time to write your novel. Or it could be the perfect time to do something else so that later when you're wide awake you can write.

Go through your day this way and push yourself to find nuggets of time to write. An excellent book on how to organize your time is Ted Schwarz's *Time Management for Writers* (Writer's Digest Books, 1988).

3.6 Save Hours (or Possibly Years) on the Phone

Jot down notes on what you plan to cover when calling an editor, expert, or other writer. Keep your call under three minutes. Chatting with friends on the phone is entertaining, but it's also a deadly time waster.

3.7 Save Time and Money on Copies

Almost every stationery store has a rubber stamp for the word "copy." Buy one for about two dollars and, next time you write a letter, avoid a trip to the copy store to make a copy for your files (client, agent, or other interested person).

Simply generate an extra copy from your printer and stamp the top with your new stamp. At ten cents a copy for photocopies, your new stamp will be paid for in about twenty letters.

3.8   Save Time at the Copy Shop

1. Organize all your material before you leave your home office.

2. Attach yellow sticky notes to the back of the material with the number of copies needed written on them.

3. Call copy shops for pricing on copies. Keep in mind that cheap isn't always the best for you. I frequent a copy shop that charges ten cents per copy, but I get VIP treatment that I wouldn't get at a discount shop. I keep a charge account with the store and pay once a month, which is helpful for tax purposes. I use the FAX number on my correspondence, and the shop calls when I receive a FAX. And when I need to FAX a confirmation of an assignment, I don't even have to leave my office. The owner of the copy shop takes all the information over the phone, sends the FAX, and charges my account.

4. Keep a file of copies of extra material you often use. Depending on how organized you are, you may want a separate file for all often-used material.

I sometimes send photocopies of the reviews of my books when I query or when I want to be considered as a speaker at a writer's conference. A great review from *Publishers Weekly* or *Booklist* goes a long way to convince people that I do know what I'm talking about. Instead of rushing out to the copy shop, I pull them from the file. I've saved hours keeping items like these reviews on hand.

3.9 Calling About Your Query

The query with a brilliant article topic you sent four days ago to *Popular Mechanics* or *Seventeen* may be the most important thing on your mind (at the moment). However, to the editor sitting in a paper-cluttered shoe-box-size office, you are just another writer looking for work.

The good news is that editors need good writers. The bad news is if you call too soon or too often, you will be labeled a pest, regardless of how delicious your query appears.

3.10 Just the Date, Please

When calling about a query, contacting someone about a lead, or trying to track down an expert, make a note of the time and date you've called on whatever paper/disk you're using. It's businesslike to say, "When I talked to you on Friday, the 11th, we discussed . . ." If you haven't made a note, you must look back at a telephone log (if you've used one) or rack your brain for the information.

3.11 To FAX or Not to FAX, That's the Question

Sending a FAX saves time when whatever you have must be there *now*. Otherwise, a FAX instead of a letter isn't economical. This tip will probably get a few arguments because when you have a machine the cost is only the price of a phone call. However, if you FAX a letter to New York, the charges will probably exceed one dollar. If you mail that same letter, it's only twenty-nine cents. Multiply that out and you'll see the savings on correspondence that can wait a few days to get to its destination. With each FAX you send, think about your phone bill and whether it really has to get there *now*.

3.12 Save Time, Save Money by Saying "No"

If you can learn to drop just one minor activity today, you will become a better worker instantly. Even if it's just skipping one low-priority luncheon, a nonessential trip to the copy store, or a ten-minute telephone gab session with a friend, you'll have more time to pursue the things that will bring you success.

Every extra minute you can save is extra money you could be making through writing.

3.13 Every Writer on Deadline Should Know Murphy's Law

In *Time Management for Writers,* Ted Schwarz talks about the Murphy's Law for Writers.

He explains: "It is a rule that the closer you get to deadline, the fewer people you will be able to reach for interviews. Call and make interview arrangements the moment you have an assignment. If you are working on speculation, do all the interviews in as short a period of time as you can.

"When you begin writing you do not want the interruption of trying to run down a source. The Murphy's Law for writers states that the availability of interview sources is directly related to the time you have to work."

3.14 Turning Interviews into Topics for Future Articles

Every time you interview someone for an article, think about how you can recycle that same interview or expert for another project. Sometimes you can use a sentence or two of what he or she said to validate your point or add an anecdote. Or, as you interview, specifically ask questions that could turn the interview into an entirely different article. You may have to get a second approval to write the next article, but the interviewing portion could be complete if you select your questions with care and an eye to saving time.

For example, while interviewing an actress for a celebrity piece, you might ask her about the sports, hobbies, or charities in which she's involved. You might luck out and discover that she spends time and energy with kids who have AIDS (a noble human-interest piece), that she's a gourmet cook (knockout idea for any of the women's magazines or food/garden journals) or that she has a mean backhand or swings that racket almost as well as Chris or Martina (*Tennis* magazine, anyone?).

If you do a lot of interviewing, keep a brief record of each person you talk with, including the date, telephone number, topic of interview, and of course the cassette tape or transcribed interview along with an interview release. In a spare minute or two (or when you're doing something else like waiting in traffic or in your dentist's office), jot down titles and topics for other articles using the basis of that same interview. Attach these notes to the file, then, as always, move as quickly as possible to get the query in the mail.

3.15 How Long Does It Take to Write a Book? Or an Article?

How much time should you estimate to write? That depends on your speed as a writer. Some writers produce two or three good pages a day and feel accomplished. The quicker you work the more money you can make . . . but you must keep quality high or you won't get more work. Remember, if you write just one page a day, everyday, in one year you will have a manuscript that's 365 pages long. If you write a page a day for five days, you'll have a thousand-word article that's ready to submit.

If you haven't guessed it yet, there's never a best time to write. If you're a night person, know it and use that time effectively. If you're like me and turn into a pumpkin with a head full of seeds after spending more than eight hours facing that blue (or amber or black) computer screen, give yourself the night off and start fresh again the next day.

Recognize that there will be times when it is absolutely impossible to write well, but you can get a lot of organizational "busy" work done, like cleaning up files on your disk and in the cabinet, straightening the books in your library, and reorganizing your office for more efficiency.

3.16   Cutting Drafts in Half

If you find you continue to rewrite and rewrite a piece, try this: Write the article or book chapter; print it out; let it sit if you have time (see below); *then* work on the draft.

Lots of writers find that they do drafts more quickly on the computer screen, but that they do more revisions, too. An obvious time waster. With a hard copy in hand, revise what needs to be revised, then go back to the computer and input your changes. Give it a quick read. You should be finished.

Be sure to put it through the spell check before you print a final copy. Typos creep into the best typed material.

3.17   Use the Freezer Technique

If at all possible allow your query or manuscript to "chill"—overnight (for a short piece), a week (for an article), or up to a month (for a book-length project). This does two things: It lets you find typos you may not have seen and it provides a fresh eye to your work so you can edit it.

3.18   Freeze with a Writer Friend

If you're just not good at finding your own typos or literary blunders, swap manuscripts with another writer. Be sure to ask before you correct or make recommendations on the prose. This can be a touchy topic unless you know exactly what you are to look for when reading a manuscript.

3.19   Getting Answers from Agents, Editors, and Publishing People

Sometimes you have to call agents, editors, and all who make up the world of publishing. Like you, these people are too busy, have tough days, and must commute to work on congested streets.

The tip here is:

• Know exactly what you want to talk about before you call. Jot down notes. Even the best of writers get nervous or tongue-tied at times.

• Ask to whom your call should be routed, and ask for the spelling of that individual's name and his or her position. You'll probably need this information so you can send a thank-you note.

• Be polite and upbeat. Try smiling when you talk. People can sense a frown, even through a telephone connection.

• Keep it professional. "Is this a convenient time to call?" "I only have two short questions and will need about three minutes. Do you have time now or shall I call another time?" "May I call when you're not in a meeting?"

• Watch your watch. If you say you're only going to talk three minutes, make it three minutes. If you suddenly realize you have something more to say (or sell), ask if you can call back or write a letter regarding the topic.

3.20   FAX Back and Get a Quicker Response

George Sheldon, author of *Preparing Effective Query Letters* and *Get Your Book Published* (both published by Archer Publications) and publisher of a monthly international newsletter *Book Writers Market Letter,* gives great advice on getting a quick response. "The one marketing trick I use is a FAX-Back Form that I have developed." George self-syndicates articles to newspapers and he says, "The form allows the editor to order my pieces quickly and easily. It allows the editor to also order other writing or pieces from me."

The FAX-Back Form consists of George's name and FAX number, and a checklist includes boxes to be marked: send material, contact him, have him call, and send more info.

"I've also added a line on the form: I know you are as busy as I am and I developed this form to try to make it easier for you. I wish someone would have given me a form like this.

"I try to be courteous and businesslike. It's a big part of what I do to sell my work. I think these words really tell an editor how I will try to do everything I can to make their job easier and not to cause any problems.

"The technique works. Since including this with my queries, I have seen about a thirty-five percent increase in sales. Too many writers forget they are running a business. Everything you can do to make it easier to do business with you is just smart."

3.21   A Right Way to Organize an Office

The furniture will arrive tomorrow, you've given your elderly desk to a favorite charity's thrift store, and now it's decision time. Basically the best way to set up your office is no secret. Place the things you use most often near you.

A secretary's chair with wheels could save you time. Buying the reference books you use most often will save you trips to the library. A telephone with a long cord between the base and the receiver will allow you to walk around the office, perhaps doing other things when you're on hold.

Don't neglect the fact that your office must be a pleasant place to work. Hang pictures, put up a bulletin board, set a photo of your kids on your desk. I frame and hang the covers of my books. They impress me. If you like music to work by, bring in a radio. This is your space.

Make it comfortable, too, with a big chair to sit in while you edit or research. Keep the temperature stable, too. If it's too cold or too hot, you will have a problem. Here in the beach city of Carlsbad, California, we do not need air-conditioning even in the summer; however, in August my office gets stuffy by midafternoon. A circular ceiling fan has been a lifesaver. It takes up no room, is quiet, and looks attractive.

If you work at home, as I do, guard against using your office (even if it's a desk in your bedroom) as a holding pen for the junk that has outgrown other rooms. And one final suggestion: make sure your office has a door. Sometimes writers need privacy; most of the time they need a large helping of it.

SECTION
4

The Power of the Printed Word—Reading, Writing, and Rejection

"Read what you write," is the best advice around on how to focus and produce publishable words. Whether you're working on a thriller or a Cajun cookbook read other books in the genre you're writing in. Constantly reading a different genre could be undermining your best intentions.

A writer of Regency romances (a formula genre) was having one heck of a time writing a novel, and her deadline was looming. It was her twenty-fifth book so she obviously knew how to produce them. However, without warning, the heroine would conduct herself in an unfitting manner for an aristocratic young lady of 1810, and the dialogue was often out of character for both the heroine and the hero.

After weeks of rewriting and hoping against hope that she hadn't lost her touch, the writer realized the real problem. Instead of spending the evening with Regency romances (as she always had in the past while writing her previous novels), she was reading one murder mystery per night and at least two science fiction novels on the weekends. Once she got back to reading what she was writing, the deliciously young heroine was returned to being more sugar than spice, and the dialogue reflected the restrained morality of the early 1800s in England.

Again, if you're having trouble writing, start to read books and articles in the style or genre you want to write; you're writing life will be easier. And since every genre has its own format, you must stay within the guidelines of what the reader expects to read.

Now let's discuss more issues on reading and writing.

4.1   Are You Guilty of "That" Abuse?

Or do you abuse other words like "so," "but," ad nauseam? As a writer who must control the runaway "thats" that sneak into my manuscripts, I can empathize. However, adding unnecessary or repetitive words takes time and can make your work less professional. A rule of thumb (as well as a trade secret) is to carefully control that addiction. Do not use two of the same memorable or colorful verbs or adjectives in the same piece if possible, definitely not in the same paragraph.

> "With every move, the moonlight bounced off the scarlet sequins of her skin-tight gown. But the costume's skin-tight enticement was wasted on her spouse, snoring in the over-stuffed chair."

The skin-tight is provocative the first time, the second should be replaced. How about body-clinging, painted-on, hip-hugging . . . you get the picture.

As you edit a manuscript, keep a watchful eye out for word abuse. For fun, do a word search on the words you use too often. You're creative—think of some other way to say the same sentence.

4.2   When Golden Words Must Go, Do It Quickly

We all have our writing foibles. *One* of mine—that isn't revealed in the polished copy that goes to an editor or appears in this book—is that at times my writing is just too sweet. Phrases rhyme and adjectives effervesce. Once in a while, it's as sweet as double Dutch chocolate cake with two inches of mocha frosting (ah, you see that did slip through, but as an example only). I really have to guard against this failing, or my reader will begin to feel bilious.

Don't think you're deficient if you, too, suffer from composing sentences that are all too smug, cute, gushy, pretentious, or eloquent. The tip here is knowing that if any words or sentences do not carry the theme of your piece, are not in the same voice as the entire manuscript, or are absolutely, positively, breath-takingly beautiful, you should probably center that curser and hit the delete key. Most likely, they're not right. Cut them out.

Sure it's painful; surgery often is. But put yourself in

your editor's chair for a minute. He or she wants you to do the "dirty" work. That's your job. When you clean out the garbage, you'll be more proficient and your editor will appreciate a professionally prepared manuscript.

4.3   Read Your Manuscript Aloud

Those who write for television, the movies, and radio have a jump ahead of writers who write for the eye only. They read everything they write out loud. This is an excellent method for any writer. In a matter of minutes you could discover that some of your words are unnecessary and/or awkward, sentences are too long, or you've rhymed the final three words.

4.4   Always Read for a Reason

College creative writing instructor Wendy Haskett, whose work has appeared in the *Los Angeles Times, Reader's Digest,* and *Glamour,* says, "Always review the small boxes at the end of articles in popular magazines. Magazines buy ideas—you don't even have to write the entire article to be paid. For example, *Woman's World* has many departments which request details for article topics. If the magazine buys your ideas, you're paid one hundred dollars or more."

4.5 Finding Just the Right Quote

Sometimes you need an authoritarian voice to validate what you have in mind. It's tough to go wrong with Harriet Beecher Stowe, super salesman Zig Zigler, Barbara Bush, or Billy Joel. The point is to select a quote that your readers can relate to and that will substantiate your thesis. Like a pinch of oregano in spaghetti sauce, the right quote or two add zest; too many, and the end result is spoiled.

4.6 How to Get a Celebrity for Your Book's Foreword

Having an expert, celebrity, or authority write the foreword for your book can make it more marketable. But how can you get this notable person when the book's still in the proposal stage? You don't have to—yet.

Begin to contact people (even the pie-in-the-sky choices) you'd like to write the foreword, and in your proposal tell the publisher who you have contacted. By the time you get the contract you'll have more of an enticement for the celebrity or authority. You can say, "Paragon House and I are most anxious for you to write the foreword."

4.7 How to Get Authorities to Contribute a Few Words for Your Book

Ask. When writing *Trade Secrets,* I wanted to sprinkle the advice of some of writing's hardest workers among the tips and suggestions in these pages. I contacted those individuals who I knew had something pertinent to say, offering only "fame and glamour of being included in this book" (i.e., lots of thanks but no payment for their words). The result was incredible. Everyone I asked laughed, then said yes.

When writing a consumer book on breast cancer awareness, *Diana's Gift,* I used the same approach. Among those who offered words of encouragement was Supreme Court Justice Sandra Day O'Connor.

Again, if you need an expert or authority, it only costs twenty-nine cents postage to write an enticing letter asking for assistance. Your local library often is great help in getting the authority's address; sometimes you have to play Sherlock Holmes, but addresses of celebrities, authorities, and experts are available.

4.8 Writing the End First

Have you ever slaved over a first paragraph or first chapter, grinding your teeth, cracking your knuckles? Join the crowd. To avoid that, try writing the end of the article or book first. Or write the beginning, give it a break, and go on to the second portion of your project.

There's a ninety-nine percent chance that when you return, it'll suddenly come back together.

4.9   Know Your Audience

As you analyze the book and magazine market, formulate exactly who your reader is. Write for this person. Identify the composite person or persons. This is important.

I write for MaryJane Peters in Kankakee, Illinois. I know a lot about this mythical woman. She reads *People* magazine and watches television, especially the news. She has a husband who is a blue-collar worker, three kids, a clerical job, little time, and cares deeply about keeping her family healthy, medical breakthroughs, and the environment. She looks for inexpensive ways to have fun. I write for MaryJane because MJ and all her sisters are the people who buy the type of books I write.

Mystery writer John D. MacDonald produces one best-selling novel after another in paperback. His books never appear in hardcover first. When one finally did, he told an interviewer how concerned he was. He shocked the reporter with "My audience is the $3.95 reader." He was successful because he knew to whom he was writing. He knew his customers.

4.10 Learn to Love Outlining

Well, maybe not "love," but to tolerate it, try these tips from Cory J Meachen with *San Diego Writers Monthly*.

- For writers who hate outlines but work better with them, start with the journalist's trick of jotting down "the five Ws and the H." Keep it short—a page, max—even for a whole book. WHO are you writing about? WHAT are they doing/have they done? WHEN, WHERE, WHY, and HOW did they/will they do it? This technique works equally well as a jumping-off point for both fiction and nonfiction projects of any length.
- Write the dustjacket blurb first. Imagine yourself browsing through a bookstore, picking up your book, reading the blurb. What needs to be there, crammed into no more than a few paragraphs, to make you buy that book? Keep what you come up with. It will be invaluable when the time comes to synopsize your manuscript for a proposal or to "sell" to agents and editors at the next conference.

4.11 Browsing Power

Browse through the supplemental sections of your telephone book, dictionary, thesaurus, and *Bartlett's Familiar Quotations* (or other favorite quotation book). You'll be astounded by the amount of useful information—and the number of potential article ideas—at your finger tips. There are maps with time zones; calendars of events; foreign words and phrases; geographical data; measurement-conversion tables; members of the United Nations; etc.

For example, here in San Diego there is the Antique Steam Engine Museum, which could be the subject for an excellent Americana article for *Country Living* or *Practical Homeowner*. Lots of cities and towns have frontier museums, religious festivals, fiestas, and traditions that are perfect magazine-article material. And when you begin to research and visit the museum, you'll also be able to locate an on-site expert there by talking with a museum docent or manager.

4.12   Buy Thank-you Notes by the Train Load

For a number of quick-witted, successful writers, this tip is one of their favorites: Send thank-you notes.

Keep a box handy and dash one off anytime anyone does anything beyond even the feeblest call of duty, including agents and publishers who personally reject your manuscript and fellow writers who pass on a referral or make an introduction.

Writing in longhand is more personal, but any computer font will do if your handwriting is as atrocious as mine. Practice feeding a card through your printer to see if it will even work; sometimes printers don't like card stock.

One writer I know uses thank-you notes made of recycled paper; it's politically correct and adds a nice caring touch. I keep a varied supply, from notes with dogs and flowers to embossed cards appropriate for more formal thank yous.

Get in the habit. People appreciate being thanked for their time and effort.

4.13   Find That Research Book *Again* Fast

Make a photocopy of the cover of any library or borrowed book you think you may need to use again, and make a note on how to locate it (e.g., with the Dewey Decimal Number or the individual from whom you borrowed it).

4.14   Has Your Book Been Rejected? You're in Great Company

Got the rejection blues? Rejection is a fact of the writing life. However, don't let it get to you or stop you from resubmitting your work.

For your information, suitable for copying and framing, here are some examples of amazing mistakes made by book editors when they evaluate manuscripts.

Why not mentally add your nonfiction work or novel to this list?

Rejected by six publishers:
Kon-Tiki by Thor Heyerdahl
Jonathan Livingston Seagull by Richard Bach
MASH by Richard Hooker

Rejected by twelve or more publishers:
The Good Earth by Pearl S. Buck
Peyton Place by Grace Metalious
Auntie Mame by Patrick Dennis
The Doctor's Quick Weight-Loss Diet by Irwin Stillman
Dubliners by James Joyce (rejected by twenty-two publishers)
The Godfather by Mario Puzo (rejected by several top publishers, then purchased with a five thousand-dollar advance. It sold more than fifteen million copies and was made into a major motion picture, with plenty of sequels.)

4.15 Millions of Dollars of Research on What Magazines Buy Is at Your Finger Tips

Some writers pour over magazine articles, counting the quotes, figuring up the statistics, keeping tabs on the amount of words in the piece. They keep a log, they analyze the masthead, they finally get ready to write. *Then* they have to determine what the magazine will buy. If this system is working for you, continue.

Like a lot of other writers, I use a (timesaving) method that's provided free of charge by the advertisers in magazines. These same companies pay Madison Avenue firms outrageous sums to determine what we, as consumers, want.

Here's what to do to cash in on their "free" service:

1. Scrutinize every advertisement.
2. Make a list of the ads that appeal to you most and what is featured in them. For example, if there are ads for cruise lines, gourmet chocolate, or exercise equipment you personally find interesting (or know others do), write this down. Leave enough room below each summary so you can write.
3. After each advertisement's summary, write three or four topics that people who use the product might want to read. For instance, those interested in cruise lines might like to read about nonwrinkling formal clothing, electrical appliances like hair dryers that can be used worldwide, and where the hottest spots to cruise will be in the next five years.
4. You now have a topical list of potentially marketable query ideas.
5. Write and sell the query. Write the article, then rewrite it or sell it again to a noncompeting publication.

If you need more info on how to find ideas to use, review my second book for this writer's series, *Writing and Selling Magazine Articles*. Recognize that you don't have to do the research. Manufacturing companies and advertising firms have done it for you, if you know what to look for.

4.16 Stop Wasting Money with Copyrights

Every time you write something and put your name on it, it's automatically copyrighted. That's the law. Often new writers think they must send money to the United States Copyright Office to protect their rights. As any adult knows, the government never turns down money, but you needn't buy a service that's unnecessary.

If you must, add a "c: Your Name" on the front or final page of your manuscript. Recognize, too, that ideas and titles cannot be copyrighted. You could call an article on the tricks of swapping baseball cards *Trade Secrets* and would be perfectly free to do so.

However, if you write plays or screenplays, when you're ready to market your work, you may want to contact the Writer's Guild and register your idea.

4.17 Quick Quote Laws You Need to Know

Without getting permission, anyone may use a small portion, five hundred words or less, of any copyrighted work as long as the individual who wrote it gets credit. The key words here are "small portion." If you're quoting a line of a poem and the poem is only two hundred words, you may not use the entire poem. A small portion would probably be less than twenty words.

However, sometimes it pays to ask permission. You may get a quote from the famous person you're citing or permission to use other material.

4.18 Money-saving Tips on Researching

There are a number of excellent books on how to research. Learn the skill and apply the techniques to all your writing assignments. These will save you energy, time, and money.

1. Look beyond the books on the library or bookstore shelf for the information you need. University and medical center libraries are usually open to writers, sometimes with special permission. Ask for it if you need the material, and/or ask their reference librarian for help.

2. Always check *Books in Print*—a multi-volume guide of all books currently available for sale—for information on your topic. These reference manuals are available at most libraries, where you can also request that a book be obtained from another library through an interlibrary loan.

3. As you research, use only the table of contents and/or the index. If a book doesn't have a comprehensive table of contents or a good index, or if you can't locate what you want by this method, do not go further with that book.

4. When researching, never read the entire book. Go directly to what you need, read it, and find the facts.

5. If you begin to falter for information about what you are writing, you may not have done sufficient research. Return to the library or bookstore, read

and review. Ask the librarian for help; these people are incredibly smart and waiting to assist you.

4.19 Time- and Money-saving Ways to Prepare for Writing

You've done your homework. You've researched the topic so that you feel confident. You know how you'd like to handle the book or article. Your next step (most likely accomplished simultaneously) is to begin preparation.

Unless you're already an expert on the topic, it's past time to read everything available on the subject on which you're expected to write. Immediately go to the library and make fast friends with the reference librarians. They love to help serious writers.

Take a trip to a large bookstore and seek out books on the same topic you'll be writing about. It might be wise to build a budget. Keep all your receipts—these verify your tax deductions for the IRS.

As you begin writing you'll profit by this initial crash-course education and have the material available should you be required to footnote, quote, or contact authorities.

There are some writers who refuse to read what the competition's written for fear of subconsciously plagiarizing it. However, by reading other books, you'll see how and where they fall short on information, and you'll be able to make yours even better or give it a slightly different slant or marketing hook. Also check the references cited in these books. They could lead you to some otherwise little-known source of information.

Keep a list of the material you use (or as suggested above, photocopy the cover of all books and articles used and include how to locate them again). Some time back I wrote a query to sell an article on the Burma Shave Sign story. Do you remember those bright yellow signs dotting the Midwest? It took months to sell the idea, then horror of horrors I couldn't locate the library book with some wonderful anecdotes I had hoped to include in the article. The only thing I could remember was that the reference book was thin and bright yellow with black writing on the spine. Yes, you've guessed it. I spent hours walking around my public library looking for that book, praying that it wasn't on loan. I finally found it and have never allowed this to happen again.

If you have any doubt that you might need any book or article as a reference when you're writing, or for future articles or books, keep some type of record—on your computer, in a card file, on a note at the bottom of your copy of the query.

4.20 *Writer's Digest* and *The Writer's Handbook* Can Get You More Work

Would you like to get some writing work without writing even a query? Then take a browse through *Writer's Digest* and *The Writer's Handbook*. Some publishers and magazine editors are most interested in receiving résumés and/or clips from writers. They want to know what you do and if your expertise is compatible with upcoming assignments. Read the entries in these reference books carefully and provide exactly what is requested.

Also, if you're using last year's book, donate it to the library and buy a new one. You're missing some sales opportunities. And when you get the new book spend a few hours browsing through it, making notes in the pages (this is your book), and follow up on leads immediately.

4.21 Paying to Have Your Work Evaluated

That's a difficult concept. If our work is good enough, we shouldn't have to pay anyone to read it. But sometimes we need to have an unbiased, professional opinion. Consider the qualifications of the evaluator, the cost, and what you will receive for the fee before you contract with the editor or evaluator.

4.22 Agents and Reading Fees. Are They Ethical?

Some agents charge a reading fee; some don't. Looking at this from a literary agent's view, it makes sense to charge a small amount (one hundred dollars or so) for the time he or she takes to read a manuscript. On the other hand, the Independent Literary Agents Association (the premier agents group) frowns on the practice.

Before you write that check, find out just what you're going to get. There's a well-known literary agent who makes an excellent living asking for money to revise the manuscript, and even more to send your work to publishers.

A more cost-effective method of getting a valuable critique might be to join a writer's workshop or creative writing class.

4.23 How to Critique Your Own Work

It's not always easy to objectively review your own work. But here are a few ways to do it:

1. Make a list of each component in your manuscript. Give yourself a grade as to how the component has been executed. For example, on a book proposal you'll have the components of a hook to get the reader interested; an overview of the book project; author's qualifications; the sample chapter; typographical errors; neatness; layout; etc. If your final averaged score is only a "C," rewrite it. You can do "B+" work without even trying and get an "A" if you put more effort into it.
2. Put your manuscript away for a few days (see "Use the Freezer Technique"). Then without looking over your work, read it aloud. If it reads smoothly, if you've covered all the points you need, and if you still like it, get it in the mail.

3. Read your work into a tape recorder. You're not being judged on your personality but on how the manuscript flows. Using this method, you'll also hear where you may need an example or anecdote or a place that's crying out for a colorful adjective.

4.24 There's Danger in Letting a Loved One Read Your Work

Even if you have an ego like Napoleon, it could be dangerous to have a loved one critique your work. Don't do it, even if he or she is a Pulitzer Prize–winner.

Unless you know exactly what you'll get from this intimate critique, you could end up with hurt feelings and a dented self-image. If you do go ahead and offer to let your loved one read your prepublished work, two things could happen: (1) you'll get a biased opinion ("Darling, I love you and your writing") or (2) you'll get an opinion of someone who isn't qualified to judge your genre ("Don't mind if I rip this to shreds, do you, Darling? There are just, oh, five hundred words which I'd like to correct").

Even those of us with tough hides can be deflated by the critical words of someone we love and respect. Instead, either critique your own work, as above, or network with other writers in your genre and exchange manuscripts.

4.25   Let's Talk About the "F" Word . . . You're Fired from a Writing Assignment or Collaboration

In every lifetime there's some measure of disappointment. If it hasn't found you yet, congratulations. Most writers have spent time slamming down a fist, crying at their computer, or wandering around the home office in a blur of disillusionment. If you're rejected, fired from an assignment, or asked to stop work on a collaborative book, take heart because most writers have been there before.

Here are some things to do instead of pouting or shouting:

- Get busy on another project.
- Make a list of everything you've ever wanted to write about and put the items in a priority order. Then write straight down that list.
- Refrain from making public comments about whoever rejected you. Don't wallow. You don't have enough energy to wallow and work at the same time.
- Keep the contact alive. If you can't say something nice, don't say anything on the subject, but don't burn your bridges either. Publishing is a small community with a long memory.
- Take a class or a workshop.
- Drop into the college creative writing class for just an hour or two (with the professor's permission, of course).

• Take the afternoon off.

• Write your feelings in a journal. That anger and/or outrage could make great material for your next novel.

• Volunteer at an Alzheimer's home, in a ghetto, with AIDS victims, or with the severely disabled. Suddenly your own lot in life will look considerably brighter.

4.26   Now a Word from the Coach

"It's not whether you get knocked down. It's whether you get up again," said football coach Vince Lombardi.

If you write for a living, you'll get knocked down. Sometimes getting rejected is painful—bruised egos and all that—but the alternative is to lie there never really knowing if you could have made it.

4.27   Sometimes You Just Need an Attitude Adjustment

"Put a few writers together and sooner or later the conversation will turn to that old bugaboo usually referred to as 'dealing with rejection,'" says Kentucky writer and member of the American Society of Journalists and Authors Nancy S. Grant, author of numerous books including *Old Glory: A History and Celebration* and *Christmas in America* (Random House) and scores of magazine articles.

"Yes, I've been disappointed when an editor says, 'no thanks' to one of my proposals, but I learned very early in life not to dwell on such things or take them personally. What I proposed simply didn't fit that editor's needs; I've got plenty more ideas, either to propose to that editor or to another one.

"I try to keep in mind what happened when I decided to put up a new fence around the horse pasture. I invited three fencing contractors to prepare a proposal and I chose the one who seemed to have the right combination of experience, the best materials, and the time to do the job when I needed it completed.

"I doubt very seriously if the two people who didn't get the job spent more than two minutes pondering why they didn't win the contract. They were far too busy organizing the job they did have and creating new proposals, a strategy that I highly recommend to writers wishing to keep the blues away and put more green in their wallets. Not very romantic, to be sure, but I prefer to apply my emotions where they'll do the most good, bringing passion and understanding to the jobs I do get, and allowing me to make that vital connection with the reader."

4.28 Samples of Forms You Should Have on Disk

You're in business. You need invoices, releases, letters of commitment, etc. You can rush down to the stationery store and try to buy them. Or you can save some money and make them yourself. You might want to use a graphic from your computer to dress 'em up.

If you have a high-tech computer system, work one up. If you're using a word processing program, like WordPerfect, just keep them simple.

For contracts, letters of intent, collaboration agreements, and releases for photographers and indexers, see *Ghostwriting: How to Get into the Business* (Paragon House, 1991).

Sample Invoice

Invoice

To:
From:
Date:
For:
Total:

(I always include a line at the bottom of invoices such as: "Thank you for your business," or "It's a pleasure working with you." Depending on your client, you might want to insert a pithy quote from Mark Twain or Dorothy Parker or an appropriate cartoon (see Keep a Smile File, below).

Sample Interview Release

This is to be typed on your stationery. If you plan to pay the subject of your interview, state so in the release. If this is an exclusive interview, include that fact, too.

Date:

I, _____ (add name of person to be interviewed), give _____ (your name) permission to use my interview dated _____ in an article (or book or anthology, etc.) called _____ .

I understand I will receive no money for my participation in this interview.

Signed:

Sample Résumé

Some writers use résumés, others don't. I find it's convenient to keep one on my computer's hard disk, print it out, and send it off. It summarizes my experience in a one-page format. Double-check for typos and keep it current. If you have yet to sell a book or magazine article, outline other germane qualifications. If you have unique qualifications, advanced degrees, or special abilities, be sure to list them. If you're a graduate from the School of Hard Knocks, you may want to include business or practical experience. For example, if you plan to write for the boating magazines, one outstanding qualification would be that you've lived aboard a twenty-two-foot sailboat for ten years and captained yachts every winter in the Bahamas.

Name, address, phone, FAX on top (or use letter head stationery).

List your published work in straight or reverse chronological order. Keep book and magazine credits separate. Your entries will look like:

"60 Fitness Ploys," *Weight Watchers Magazine,* June 1991.

"Salute to the Kernel," *Westways Magazine,* May 1991.

"Networking How-To's," *Entrepreneurial Woman,* April 1991.

Diana's Gift, University of California, San Diego, 1992.

Writing and Selling Magazine Articles, Paragon House Publishers, 1992.

Ghostwriting: How to Get into the Business, Paragon House Publishers, 1991.

Sample Letter of Confirmation for Magazine Assignment

Use your best business letter-writing style. Include the topic of the article, the word count, the due date, possible kill fee (if the article is not used), what rights are to be purchased, and your fee for writing the article, plus when it is to be paid. Be sure to confirm other relevant details such as reimbursement for expenses. With your return address on top, or using letterhead, it might sound like:

Name, address of editor/magazine

Dear Ms. Jones:

This letter will confirm our telephone conversation today regarding my assignment to write an article for *Southern Living,* tentatively titled "Grandma's Five-Ingredient Chocolate Cake." I understand that the magazine will be purchasing first North American Serial Rights, the kill fee (if necessary) is fifty percent of the assigned payment, and I will receive $900.00, when the article is accepted for publication.

As we discussed, the article will run approximately

one thousand words, the due date is October 15, and I will be reimbursed for telephone and travel expenses of no more than $150.00. If the photo I submit is used, I will receive $100.00 for one black-and-white photo of Grandma Violet Adams, Marge Adams North (my mother), myself, and my daughter Delta making the cake in Grandma's nostalgic Atlanta kitchen.

Please let me know if you have any questions or if there are items I have inadvertently omitted from this letter. I would appreciate your signing this letter and returning a copy in the enclosed SASE.

Looking forward to sharing Grandma Adams's scrumptious recipe with *Southern Living* readers.

Sincerely,

Sample Manuscript Format

For complete book manuscript format and submission suggestions, refer to David Carroll's *How to Prepare Your Manuscript for a Publisher* (Paragon House Publishers, 1988).

For magazine articles, always:
- Single space your name, address, and phone number on the top right corner of the first sheet of the manuscript.
- Center the title with your name directly below it.
- Place the page number either in the center at the bottom or with the tag line (the title of the manuscript and your name) at the top of the second and subsequent pages.
- Double-space the manuscript, indent paragraphs five spaces, try to get about two hundred to two

hundred forty words per page, using a dark type style from your printer. Dot matrix is not appropriate.

- You may want to fasten the sheets together with a clip. Some editors like staples, others don't. It's a coin toss. I sometimes fold a small (recycled) piece of paper over the top left corner of the manuscript and slip a paper clip over everything. It looks neat and keeps everything together.
- You may also want to type your name, address, phone, and FAX on the last page of the manuscript.

Sample Query

Make it punchy and to the point. Use your best writing style. You have about five seconds to get your point across to the editor. Try to keep your query to one page. Try to keep it in three paragraphs, no more than four.

Here's a 1, 2, 3 format I've found consistently successful:

On letterhead or with your name, address, phone, and FAX at the top of the paper, type the date and inside address (that's the editor's name, address, etc.).

If you can't figure out the gender of your editor, start with "Good morning," or leave an extra line and begin your letter. The numbers in parentheses indicate paragraphs.

Dear Mr./Mrs./Ms./Good morning:

(1) Hit 'em with something quick, provocative, or meaty. Add name of article or book, even if it's a working

title, so that when the assignment is confirmed you both know exactly what you're talking about.

(2) Explain why you are qualified to write on this topic, your connection to the individual who is to be interviewed, or whatever appropriate information that will get you the work. Continue with a brief outline of what is to be covered in the article.

(3) Close with a sentence or two, mentioning the SASE that's enclosed and (if requested) clips of your work.

For more tips on query letters, review Paragon House's *Writing and Selling Magazine Articles* and Lisa Collier Cool's *How to Write Irresistible Query Letters* (Writer's Digest Books).

4.29   Cover Letters for Transmission of Books and Articles

Don't make the cover letter complicated. It is there to "cover" your manuscript. Mention that the manuscript has been requested, if it was. Make sure you have an SASE in there, too.

4.30   The Power of the P.S.

Anything you add as a postscript will be read. Make use of this trade secret to hit home your point.

For example, let's say you're querying *Rolling Stone* magazine for an article about your life as a "roadie" (one who travels before or with a musical group to accomplish all the technical preparation and make the performance happen). An eye-catching postscript might be: "PS: Enclosed is a snapshot of Mick Jagger and me before his performance at Madison Square Garden." If that doesn't get the editor's attention, little will.

4.31   Everything You Should Know About Editorial Etiquette

If only Emily Post had a manual on editorial etiquette, then as writers we might not feel so perplexed about what's proper, what's not. However, to get you thinking in this direction, keep these trade secrets in mind.

1. You only get one shot with publishers on a book submission *unless* the editor has specifically recommended that you make certain changes and suggests that you resubmit the proposal and/or manuscript. If it's rejected, it's futile to send the manuscript back three months later.

2. If you change literary agents while a book is being marketed to publishers, always be truthful with the new agent. Tell him or her where the book manuscript has been marketed, what transpired with each publisher, and why you changed agencies.

3. Forego the temptation to tell your new agent that your former agent ("that #$$#! did this and that!") isn't fit to shine an editorial assistant's shoes.

A difference of opinion, a change in your literary direction, and the time to find a more aggressive (cultured, passive, etc.) agency are all acceptable reasons to change. Once you and the new agent become chums, then cautiously display whatever dirty laundry is pertinent to the relationship. Until then, keep it confidential.

4. If a query is rejected by a magazine editor but accompanied by a note that you should submit it again in six months, mark your calendar and do so, unless you've sold the piece. You may want to follow up with a note or phone call asking if their editorial calendar is full or if you should submit other article ideas.

5. If a query is rejected, don't send it back to that same magazine. It didn't work the first time, it won't work the second. However, if you've sent it to the wrong editor (to the life-style editor instead of the home decorating editor), it is appropriate to resubmit it. Don't let this happen more than once; your name will get around, but not in a professional context.

6. When one of the magazines or publishers for whom you write produces something you especially like, write a fan letter to the author, the editor, and the publisher. Too often we quickly point out wrong-doings; take time to praise.

7. While it's not necessary to subscribe to the magazines you write for, it's always correct to let an editor know you're a regular reader. If your Uncle

John has been subscribing since 1942 (and it's appropriate), you may want to mention that fact, too.

8. Read the entries in *Writer's Digest, The Writer,* and the other writer's trade journals and books to keep on top of where editors are working. Since editors often move from one publishing house or magazine to another, you'll want to stay in contact with your favorites, perhaps with a note acknowledging the change or promotion.

4.32 How to Read the Entries in Writer's Magazines

Carefully review the entries in writer's magazines. Here are some checkpoints:

1. The percentage of the magazine which is free-lance written.
2. How the magazine pays (e.g. on publication or acceptance) and how long (if applicable) after publication the magazine pays.
3. How often it is published.
4. Word length compared to pay schedule.
5. Tips from the editors on how to sell to the magazine. For example, an entry for *Runner's World* might say that the best way to break into selling to this periodical is through short, humorous fillers. If

you can write amusing essays as well as more serious pieces on the sport, you've got your foot in the door.

6. Call or write for the guidelines and follow them exactly. The guidelines have been prepared to help, not stymie, us. (If you can't get copies of the guidelines or if the subject you are querying on is too timely and you can't wait, give it your best professional shot and send the query immediately. At worst you'll be totally off the mark; at best the creative approach taken will win you an assignment. . . .)

7. If the guidelines and/or entries in writer's manuals for magazines or book publishers specifically request certain information, such as clips, send whatever is asked for. Also, if a magazine or publisher says it doesn't print a certain genre (the one in which you prefer to write), don't frustrate yourself and squander your time or money to query. If they don't ever use interviews, even your up-close-and-personal conversation with Dr. Ruth isn't going to sell.

4.33 Writing Book Proposals That Sell Books

As outlined in *Ghostwriting: How to Get into the Business,* there is a book proposal (a literary/business plan to sell an unwritten book) that works, with modifications, for most books. However, there's always that exception to the rule. Some publishers prefer a specific format. If in doubt, call the publisher or your literary agent, or write for the proposal guidelines. If a specific formula is desired, the publisher will let you know.

If you're working with an agent, ask if he or she has sample proposal formats that have sold books. Your agent won't write the proposal for you, but he or she can advise you of the best format.

SECTION
5

Making Your Name Known in
All the Right Places

Before we get started on the trade secrets in this section, let's get to some basics: the 3R's—recession, rejection, and resilience.

I believe the current economic slump brings only good news for writers. Any recession separates the women from the girls, the men from the boys, the wheat from the chaff. The writing field is wide open to professional, persistent writers like us, and we can profit during tough times. Truly, by hanging in here, it will be easier to establish outstanding careers. Don't make the excuse that the times are difficult. As Woody Allen says, "Eighty percent of success is showing up." Regardless of what the Dow Jones is doing or the strength of the yen, show up for work by writing every day. The opportunities have never been better when you make your own.

The second R is rejection. In 1984, I wrote a little book called *60-Second Shiatzu,* a modified form of Japanese acupressure. The little book was rejected by forty-nine publishers—some rejected the concept, some the query, and a few rejected the entire manuscript.

The fiftieth publisher bought it, and the rest is publishing history at its best. "SSS" is in its third printing in the United States, third for a major publisher in South America, and second for Simon and Schuster who published it for distribution throughout the United Kingdom. It has just been translated into Portuguese by a Brazilian publisher, and I recently heard it will be published in Mexico, Italy, Hungary, Austria, and the Netherlands. Yesterday, I got word that there are nibbles of interest from a publisher in Germany.

I've given up trying to keep track of how many copies have sold, and this for a book that was sold without the help of a literary agent. Every year I make at least an additional thousand dollars on royalties, some years considerably more.

So if you're feeling deflated with a manuscript that's been rejected twice, or four times, or even twenty times, remember *60-Second Shiatzu,* a.k.a. my little gold mine, and don't stop until you've hit fifty.

The third R is resilience. To be a writer you have to do a lot of bouncing. You must be flexible enough to change and stretch your talents to polish your work. You must promote yourself as if you're a product. And never consider failure to be an option.

5.1 Publicize Your Book, but Don't Do It Too Soon

If your new book is coming out in June, don't do publicity before the book is actually available. Otherwise, the consumer who loves your topic, reads about the book, or sees you on television—but can't find the book in the store—will buy a competitor's book. You must become a public relations person when your book is available.

5.2   Thirteen Tips to Promote Your Book

Let's say your book is finished and it's scheduled for release next month. You're about to bust your buttons with pride and your mother has told every soul in Middletown, USA, that her favorite offspring is now a published author. That's a good start on publicity, but to continue sales you must take matters into your own hands.

1. Talk directly to the individual who is in charge of marketing and/or promotion for your publisher. Become good friends with this person. Ask what you can do. Listen. Be willing to do anything to promote your book. This takes patience and time, but it's well worth the energy since the publisher probably has more experience in this area than you.

2. Ask the publisher's PR department for a list of where sample copies and/or press releases have been sent. You won't want to copy any effort that's not meant to be duplicated, explained in the next step.

3. Ask the PR department to make up an order form/ flier with information about the book, about you,

with review quotes, etc. Have it printed on colored paper. If the publisher doesn't have a budget for this insignificant expense, do it yourself with the help of a friend who has desk-top publishing capacities.

4. Make a list of everybody you know, including college roommates, the president of the national organization you belong to, and the basketball coach of your daughter's team. (See "Make Your Own Worth-a-Million Mailing List, below.)

5. Send the order form/flier to everyone on your mailing list. This is not a sell letter. Ask that they take the flier to their local public library and the bookstore they frequent and that they inquire if the book can be added to the shelves. If you do this right, you will have hundreds of sales people out there pushing your book—at the grass roots level.

6. Personally write to all the magazines you believe would enjoy featuring or mentioning your book. Write to the book review editors of newspapers from the *Los Angeles Times* to *USA Today*. Sure your publisher may have sent a press release and/or sample copy of your book; but a personal request often gets through where a form letter doesn't.

7. Be sure to tell your local hometown paper that your book is available.

8. Make some news by donating copies of your book to the university, college, and/or high school from which you graduated. Also, give copies to your

local public library and their adult literacy program. To make news, you must have a press release and call the editor of the paper in that area to get the "hometown woman makes it as an author" angle.

9. Call or stop by your local bookstore to make sure they'll be stocking the book. Give them a flier or twenty; be sure to always carry a few around with you.

10. Volunteer to provide a program at the local library on the topic of your book, if your library offers this type of service. This, again, is news when you tell the newspaper that you're providing the program.

11. Depending on your agreement with the publisher, offer to write (free if necessary) some articles on your book's topic for publications which will appeal to your book's reader. For example, when publicizing *Ghostwriting: How to Get into the Business* I wrote an article on how to be a ghost for *San Diego Writer's Monthly,* another for a writer's magazine in Florida, and a third for *Writer's Monthly,* a London-based writer's journal, among a number of others. *Book Writer's Market Letter* featured an interview with me in exchange for a plug for my writer's books. *And* I've also bartered to write a monthly column for a small-sized writer's magazine in exchange for a half-page advertisement for the ghostwriting book.

Sure all this takes work. However, the success

of your book is far more important to you than it is to the publisher's PR department, regardless of how supportive they are.

12. For more trade secrets of publicity, review the books on this topic at your library or bookstore.

13. When doing your own publicity, remember it never hurts to ask.

5.3 Make Your Own Worth-a-Million Mailing List

When speaking at writers' conferences and to university classes, I always go prepared with a mailing list sign-up sheet attached to a clipboard. For anyone who is interested, I ask that they write their name and address on the lined tablet. I often send out mailings, such as #5 above; but in addition I have the computer list coded (along with personal notes) so fiction writers might get a clipping about a new market and those who write nonfiction may receive an amusing article. All receive fliers of my writing books.

Call it networking, grass roots aid, a helping hand, or anything you want—it gets your name out and your books sold. And the publisher will adore you. (If you want to be on my ever-growing list, send your name and address to me in care of Paragon House, and you'll be there forever.)

Patricia C. Gallagher, author of *For All the Write Reasons! Forty Successful Authors, Publishers, Agents and Writers Tell You How to Get Your Book Published*—a must-add-this-one-to-your-library reference book (Young Sparrow Press, 1992, a Writer's Digest Book Club Featured Selection)—lecturer, and super PR woman, takes the "grass roots" approach a quantum leap further. She sends out a sheet called "Easy Ways to Put Money in Your Pocket." The info sheet says that she will (happily) pay a finder's fee to the first person who succeeds in making a contact that results in an interview or feature story regarding her or her book.

The amounts for each area—from "Regis and Kathy Lee" to a mention in *Modern Maturity*—are clearly outlined. Eager-beavers can earn three hundred dollars from putting Patricia in touch with a producer who does a show about her book and a ten spot for a mention in a newsletter.

5.4 Keep a Smile File

Everybody loves to laugh; I often think writers need to more than people with "real" jobs. Start now collecting for your "smile file." When it's appropriate, attach an amusing cartoon or funny article when sending an assigned article to your editor.

One I just saw was a keeper. It shows a man in the doctor's office and the nurse reviewing a paper. She says, "Sorry, Mr. Smith, your disability policy doesn't cover writer's block."

Something from your smile file *will not* help you sell writing that's substandard, but it *will* make your submission appreciated and your name remembered. Don't go

overboard, though. Use this tip sparingly for the best effect.

5.5 Get Your Name into Thousands of Homes Absolutely Free

Contact your community college, clubs, and civic organizations and offer to teach or give a workshop. Journal writing is always a winner with seniors' groups. You may want to do it for free or charge a nominal amount. What this will do for you is publicize your new book, especially helpful if you're self-published. But don't stop there. Call

111

the life-style editor of your local newspaper and tell him/
her that you're giving this course and you have written a
book. Your success story is news. What do you get? Your
books will sell. And your name could become a household
word.

5.6   There's a Language in Writing for Specialty Publications

Specialty magazines, whether it's *Dog Fancy* or *NASA
Tech Briefs,* have their own "language." As a free-lancer,
you must understand and write in that lingo. Liz Palika,
whose work has appeared in all the popular specialty
magazines geared to the pet owner and who is the author
of *Fido, Come!* (Doral Publishing, 1993), explains, "In my
own specialty, a finish is an exercise that an obedience-
trained dog will do to put himself back into a heel
position. To a painter, a carpenter, or a person who
sharpens knives, a finish means something else entirely.

"A writer who is unfamiliar or uses the language of the
trade incorrectly marks him- or herself as an amateur or a
sloppy writer—either way that spoils the chances for
future assignments. And immediately shouts to the editor that the necessary research hasn't been done."

5.7   An Expert's Guide to Placing Poetry

Poet Cathy Colman has taught poetry at the University of California, Los Angeles, for seven years. Her work has been published in anthologies such as *New Poets: Women, Hair Raising,* and *Rohwedder Magazine.* She cuts to the quick with advice for anyone who wants to get their name known, especially those who want to do it through writing poetry.

"There's little profit in poetry today. I was on a bus in San Francisco's Chinatown once with a friend and we were talking about poetry. An elderly Asian gentleman who had been listening to our conversation interrupted us suddenly: 'Too expensive,' he said.

"I thought: Gee, he's right. It's difficult to *afford* to write poetry because it doesn't generate money itself.

"But when he continued with 'Too expensive to feed,' I knew we were on a different wave length. 'Poetry?' I questioned. " 'hat's right,' he answered nodding his head, his mouth contorted in a pensive line. 'Poultry.'

"Whether he knew it or not, that elderly gentleman was right. One cannot write poetry for money, but only for love, which I think is the only satisfying motivation for doing anything."

Cathy suggests reviewing literary magazines and journals for tips on how to publish your poetry. "It's really a numbers game. I had a student who put the addresses of the literary magazines on his computer and submitted constantly and in bulk. He was not a particularly good

113

poet, but he had over one hundred poems published *in less than two years*.

"It was once thought that the practice of simultaneous submission was bad form. Now it's considered acceptable, unless otherwise stated by the magazine. *Poets Market* and the *Directory of Small Presses and Literary Magazines,* as well as the magazine *Poets and Writers,* are all good sources for poetry." As with all submissions, Cathy recommends reading the magazine first to see if your style fits the type of poetry published.

Cathy says:

1. Do a good edit on a poem and have it printed in dark, readable type, either a laser jet or something close, will help.
2. Before you send out poems, read them out loud. If your tongue falters over a word, you should probably edit it out.
3. Editors like short cover letters. If you have published before, mention where. Thank the editor for their time and sign off. Don't fill your letter with flattery.
4. It's always good to send more than one poem. Editors, like people who shop in a bazaar, like to say no to something and yes to something else.
5. Just like all writing, you'll be rejected. That's good, however, because it means you're sending out your work and people are becoming familiar with your name. Even if they don't accept you the first

time, keep submitting, especially if an editor writes a personal note on the rejection slip.

6. Make submitting your work a regular part of your schedule. Supposedly it takes twelve submissions of the same piece before you get an acceptance. Get those envelopes out—and don't forget the SASE.

7. If a friend gets accepted into a magazine or anthology, ask if you can use their name and submit work to that publication along with a note that "so and so" suggested you do it.

8. Be aware that many small local magazines and newspapers publish poetry. Publishing anywhere is helpful.

9. Don't be afraid to send your best stuff to the big guns. You never know.

5.8   The Confession Markets—a Writer's Gold Mine

For years the as-told-to story has been the basis for women's, celebrity, sports, and news magazines. Whether you write fiction or nonfiction, these could be a gold mine if you can produce high-quality stories in a short amount of time. Take another look at *Modern Romance, True Confessions,* and *Intimacy/Black Romance.*

All the magazines have slightly different slants. Some are written for the ethnic market, some for teenagers, some for family-oriented women. They aren't just fluff; you must write excellent dialogue, have strong characters, and a plot that entertains and sometimes educates. I've written over two hundred stories for the confession market focusing on topics women can relate to: death of a parent, step-parenting, returning to work after a baby is born, the child-care disaster, etc. Some of the stories came from my own experience (any woman over twenty-five has learned a few lessons in life); some were the results of interviews with other women who have overcome obstacles. Often I changed the plot line and names to protect the privacy of those involved, yet I always explained in my cover letters that these stories were based on true incidents.

If you're a nonfiction writer trying to break into fiction, writing for the confession market can get you exactly where you want to be. Suddenly you'll have clips showing you can pull off a story, write dialogue, and portray characters that carry the plot. And keep in mind, the confessions insist on quality writing, professionally prepared. Once they like your stuff, however, you're practically one of the team. Confessions use hundreds of stories each year, plus fillers and poetry. They also use how-to articles.

5.9 Big Trouble in River City. What to Do When You Need More Time to Complete an Assignment

First, this should never happen. When accepting magazine or book assignments, project how much time you really need and extend it, if possible, by one third. Research always takes longer: people you need to interview are out of town, and/or you win Publisher's Clearing House Sweepstakes and want to spend some of the prize money in Paris, etc.

A friend who recently received her first book contract after writing for magazines for a number of years almost blew it. She fell into a trap that other writers have suffocated in. The thought process sounded good, but in actuality, theory and practice are two different things. Her idea was that if it took her a day to write a feature article of two thousand words and the book she'd contracted for was only sixty thousand words, then it should run true that she could write the book in a month. Fat chance.

We talked about time schedules and reality. It always takes much longer to write a book than a series of articles. And it always takes longer to write an article than you originally plan for. These are facts of life.

So that this doesn't happen, as mentioned above, always project your work schedule. What other articles/ books are you committed to write? Plot out your work with progress steps on a grid if that makes it easier. Again, add one third of the time to the final estimate.

If you work on a number of books and/or magazine articles at one time, it pays to always keep an assignment list handy. Include due date and other info that makes the list work for you.

Okay, you blew it. The deadline is approaching like a runaway freight train and you're tied to the track. You'll never make the deadline. First, when you initially realize you'll need an extension, double-check your work load, see if you can delegate any nonwriting work, and then figure out how to streamline your writing process. Second, if that doesn't do it, call the editor (or your literary agent for books) at the first instant you realize you might have to turn the material in late. It's far better and more professional to shriek "uncle" two months before a book is expected than the actual date it's due.

A good excuse probably won't help, but do explain what really has transpired (e.g., the subject of an interview is unavailable; Typhoon Buffy swept away your house; your computer died an excruciating death with the manuscript's only copy on the hard disk).

Make sure you're ready with a new, realistic due date, and make the date as soon as humanly possible. Sometimes this works, sometimes it doesn't. In the case of a book contract, supplying the manuscript late may well void the contract and you'll be expected to return the advance.

When you can't supply an article or a book at the specified time, you must be prepared to lose the contract. Even your wonderful, kind, and gentle editor may have to tell you sayonara. He or she has deadlines and bosses and stock holders to report to.

Be realistic. Give yourself some "cushion" time when you make a commitment to turn in a manuscript, then work like crazy if necessary to be as good as your word.

5.10 A Writer's Guide to Networking

If you want to write and sell your work, submit it. If you want more chances for success, network.

Sales people use it. Entrepreneurs use it. Store owners and crafts people use it, too. But some writers think it's not applicable to their creative efforts. Not true. Networking has become *the* established way to do business in the nineties. Smart writers access more work through this personalized method.

And there are golden opportunities in your own city. Ali Lassen, founder of the world's largest networking organization, Leads Club (based in Carlsbad, California) and author of a number of books on networking including *Power Plays* (Leads Club Publishing, 1992), offers the next trade secrets on networking specifically for writers:

In your own neighborhood, there are outstanding chances to boost your income with possible writing assignments when you network. That means you must tap into the markets for writing in your community and let your community know you write for a living. How do you do that? By networking, getting the word out, joining organizations from Young Democrats to The Committee to Save High Street.

As your name as a local writer becomes known, take it further. Could an attorney use a workbook for his/her financial planning seminars? Would your town's chiropractor do more business with a monthly newsletter or newspaper columns that also work as ads? Have you thought about collaborating with a beauty specialist for a series of articles for the women's magazines or a beauty book for the harried career woman? These people need the services of a writer—your goal is to let them know you're available.

On a national level, every time you make a sale to a magazine your network is growing. When you provide excellent material on a timely basis, you ensure a reputation as a serious writer. Therefore, ask editors to recommend you for other assignments, to other magazine editors, for upcoming projects. As you already know, editors tend to move from one magazine or publishing house to another, and if you are part of their professional network, your name and phone number will go with them.

It's a fact of life that before people will refer you and your writing services, they must know you're an ethical human being. This comes across in the confidence you show personally, the integrity in which you do business, and your professionalism.

Discover your own network. Right this second, you have more than two hundred fifty people in a personal circle . . . your own network. These are the folks who tune your car, the checker at the store, your insurance agent, and your physician, along with friends and your college pals. These people are part of your network and are potential sources for expert advice for how-to articles, individuals to feature for personality pieces and profiles, ghostwriting clients, quotes, etc. By letting these people know that you are in the writing business and asking for referrals, you will multiply your word-of-mouth advertising approach that is the core of good networking.

For business leads as well as a weekly boost of professional energy, join a networking organization. They're excellent, although writers who work with magazines and publishers often understate the value. Attend a few meetings with various groups, talk with the members, find out the scope of professions covered in the organization, and go with your intuition as to the right one to join.

Within an organized networking club, you'll have access to decorators, doctors, and gourmet chefs. You can work with these professionals as ghostwriting clients, for speech writing, or PR. You may network with someone whose profession is perfect for a feature story or a personality profile.

As you meet with potential networking team members, keep your business cards handy. One writer puts her cards in her right jacket pocket and a pen in the left. As she exchanges business cards, those from other people go into her left pocket, with a quickly jotted note, and she follows up on all potential leads before filing the cards.

Promotion made easy. Whether you join an organized networking association or network with people you already know, you must ask for business. That's as simple as saying, "Should you need the services of a writer for your in-house newsletter, I hope you'll consider me." Or, "I write for *ABC Magazine* and I know the editor would be interested in an article about someone in your profession." Then hand the individual a business card and follow up on what you say you'll do.

However, you can get more than great business from your network. If you look and listen, you'll learn how to dress for success, how to approach clients, how to promote your business, and how to speak in public. Being around winners gives you the opportunity to learn winning ways.

As your career begins to build, you may also want to surround yourself with a writer's network or group. This is not a coffee and complaint session—steer clear of the clubs that meet for chitchat. Join or establish a network of working writers to share your triumphs, help cushion the disappointments, perhaps critique your queries, and/or provide instructional programs and workshops.

When meeting and talking with writers who seem to be on the same wavelength, get a phone number; establish a business relationship. When you call, *always* make sure it's a convenient time to talk. "Are you in the middle of a sentence? Shall I call back?"

Give and you'll receive. It's a fact. As you become established in a network of writers and professionals, you must go out of your way to give referrals in order to get more. Why should you let go of any possible business when you desperately need it yourself? Simple. There's a law of the universe as certain as Newton's that the more referrals you give, the more you get. This law holds true whether you're referring another writer to a magazine's editor or a personality who you know would make an outstanding story for your city's feature editor.

As you receive referrals, always follow through by making a contact. Go the extra mile and follow up with the person who made the referrals. Explain briefly what transpired. This is not only good manners; it cements your network.

5.11 Too Much Work? Share It

It may not have happened yet, but one of these days, you'll have too many incredible opportunities for paid writing assignments. When it occurs, pass the overload to other writers rather than telling an editor you can't write the article or column. (This is inappropriate, of course, if you've queried and the magazine has accepted your suggested article.) Thus when an editor calls, offers an assignment, and you're too busy, recommend someone in your writer's organization or network.

When you refer work, immediately call the writer you've recommended to explain what transpired. "Hello, Jim. This is Margaret. I'm tied up writing my book and can't take an assignment. I've just told the editor of *Autowreckers Monthly* that you might be interested in doing an article on sculpture from scrap metal. With your art background and the six years you spent as an Indy 500 mechanic, I told her you'd be perfect."

If you want to keep the connection with the magazine open for the next assignment, be sure to write a thank-you note to the editor and continue to send queries once you know your work load. You don't want to have to pass on too many assignments, or you won't get calls.

This referral technique works well both ways. Let other writers in your network know that you're interested in referrals, tell them exactly what constitutes a good referral, and be sure to thank whoever refers you.

5.12   Tips for the Self-published Book

Patricia Gallagher has successfully self-published many books. She says, "If you are going to publish yourself, do your best to make your book look like one found on the shelves in a bookstore. Don't let it appear homemade.

"Spiral bindings may be okay for a book that you are going to sell at a seminar, but if you want 'respect,' follow the example of the major publishers with regard to size of book paper, cover design, bar code, ISBN, laminated cover, and name of book and author on the spine. See what competing books look like and follow their pattern for success.

"You must include a coupon so that people can order directly from you. Look at other books and see how they have designed an order form. I sold about one thousand copies of a book to libraries in 1987. Now, several years later, I still get requests for that book from people who saw it in the library and decided that they wanted their own copy.

"It helps to say 'satisfaction guaranteed' or 'money back' when you are selling by mail. The order coupon is included within my books both in the front and in the back."

For more timely and factual information, Patricia's book is a winner. Dan Poynter's *Self-Publishing Manual* is the "bible" for those who have successfully taken publishing into their own hands.

5.13 How to Get (at Least!) Ten Percent More on Each Book and Writing Assignment

You want to write the great magazine article or wonderful book and now your query letter has sparked a phone call from the editor. In your heart, you know you'd do it for the price suggested, but wait. Would you like a little more money? Then ask. How? Simply repeat the offered amount, adding (at least) 10 percent. This really works. I recently proved it once more when offered a substantial (in the midfive figures) advance for a book. I was offered a specific amount and asked for twenty percent more; we settled on 10 percent.

"I'm pleased that you like my proposal for *One Thousand Ways to Say I Love You*, and I appreciate your offer of $2,000, however I'd like to get at least $2,800 for the article."

Or "Will your editorial budget allow an extra $50.00 for this article on the care and feeding of citrus trees?"

You really have nothing to lose, and you have (at least) ten percent to gain.

5.14 Should You Ever Sue for Nonpayment?

Tough question. Before you decide to sue, write a stern letter asking for payment and include any documentation you may have: a letter of commitment, jotted notes, a scribble condensing the phone call when the editor offered you the work. Follow up with a phone call and another letter. Then resort to "I will turn this matter over to my attorney in thirty days unless I hear from you."

Small claims court is a good place to start if you have not received payment for an article published by a magazine or paper in your state. The fee is nominal. If you haven't received payment for a book, your agent is the first line of defense. If he or she hasn't lived up to your agreement, you may have to contact a literary attorney.

Nonpayment doesn't happen often, but it pays to keep records and know what is expected and when. In fourteen years I've been writing, nonpayment has only happened once. The realization still stings, but as Grandma would tell you, "Life isn't always fair."

5.15 Make Your Book or Face Famous

Have postcards made up with the cover of your new book and your photo on the front. On the back, leaving room for the mailing label and stamp, add publicity blurbs about your book. They are great for advanced sales, for publicizing your about-to-be-released book, and for offering to lecture and appear on television shows. They're also great as a follow up: "If you have questions on the query I sent on May 11, please give me a call."

Publicity whiz Patricia Gallagher uses them by the score and takes a highlighter pen to emphasize specific points.

5.16 Protecting Your Reputation

Most free-lance writers have, at one time or another, said they'll "do anything for a buck." This is a glib remark for the majority of us because if we're dedicated, there's nothing nonchalant about how we plan our careers. Like Hollywood actors, we are often known from the type of material we write, so while a buck in the hand is essential, we make sure that what we write reflects the writer we want to be.

Work that is shoddy, unprofessional, incorrect, or plagiarized has been the undoing of some great free-lancers. If you want to make (and keep) a name as the best writer on Mother Earth, then you must work as hard as possible to do that. As they say in the barbering trade, you're only as good as your last haircut. Choose your clients, and the types of books and magazine articles you write, with care.

5.17   A Final Trade Secret

Success is failure overcome by persistence. Success is a habit. Success is just a stamp and a query away.

I hope you'll use these trade secrets, share them, scatter them out at the next writers' conference. And if you have a few secrets you'd like to give to me, I'd like to hear them. Just write to:

Eva Shaw c/o Paragon House Publishers
90 Fifth Avenue
New York, NY 10010

Recommended Reading

Carroll, David. *A Manual of Writer's Tricks*, Paragon House Publishers, New York, NY, 1990.

Carroll, David. *How to Prepare Your Manuscript for a Publisher*, Paragon House Publishers, New York, NY 1988.

Gallagher, Patricia C. *For All the Write Reasons: 40 Successful Authors, Publishers, Agents and Writers Tell You How to Get Your Book Published.* Young Sparrow Publishing, Worcester, PA, 1992.

Griffith, Joe. *Speaker's Library of Business Stories, Anecdotes and Humor*, Prentice Hall, Englewood Cliffs, NJ, 1990.

Lassen, Ali. *Power Plays—Getting the Edge on Your Competition Through Focused Networking.* Leads Club Publishing, Carlsbad, CA, 1992.

Schultz, Dodi, and the American Society of Journalists and Authors. *Tools of the Writer's Trade*, HarperCollins, New York, NY, 1990.

RECOMMENDED READING

Schwarz, Ted. *Time Management for Writers*. Writer's Digest Books, Cincinnati, OH, 1988.

Shaw, Eva. *Ghostwriting: How to Get into the Business*. Paragon House Publishers, New York, NY, 1991.

Shaw, Eva. *Writing and Selling Magazine Articles*. Paragon House Publishers, New York, NY, 1992.

About the Author

Eva Shaw is a professional ghostwriter who has published more than one thousand books, magazine articles, newspaper columns, and speeches under her clients' bylines, plus many books and articles on which her own name appears. She is a member of the American Society of Journalists and Authors.

A resident of Carlsbad, California, Shaw says, "The tips and advice—all the trade secrets in this book—are a result of years of real-world experience. They may not make you more attractive, more intelligent, or more worldly, but they will tell you how to save time and make more money. And you can take that to the bank."

Other Paragon House books by Shaw include the best-seller *Ghostwriting: How to Get into the Business* and *Writing and Selling Magazine Articles*.